Behind the Scenes:
Managing a Trade Show
Without Losing Your Mind

Pamela Rocke

Cave Cat Press
Laguna Hills, California

Rocke, Pamela R.
     Behind the scenes: managing a trade show without losing your mind/ Pamela R. Rocke—1st ed.
     Includes bibliographical references and index.
     ISBN 0-9760957-0-X
     1. Trade shows.
     2. Marketing.

Library of Congress Control Number: 2004096793

Printed in the United States of America.

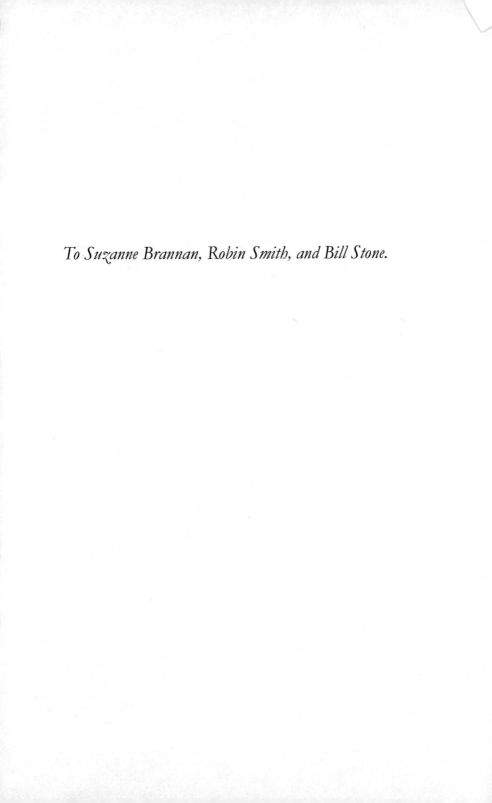

To Suzanne Brannan, Robin Smith, and Bill Stone.

Contents

Part 1 - Getting Started: Trade Show Basics

Part 2 - Fist Full of Leads: Seducing Great Prospects

Chapter 6—Calling All Prospects: How to Use Advertising and Public Relations to Maximize Your Trade Show Success 93

Part 4 - After Words

X

Acknowledgements

I especially want to thank Mike Foley for helping me with this book.

The encouragement and advice of my friends and colleagues Katherine Sartori, Cindy Cooksey, Denise Westcott, Catherine Singer, Edward M. Pallette, M.D., Beverly Ingram, Owen Jay Murphy, Ofra Obejas, Lorenzo Porricelli, Naomi Voorhees, and Leslie Williams were the foundation upon which this project was built. I am forever grateful.

Super special thanks also to Philip Reed and Martin J. Smith.

Thanks also to Mike Boschma—the ultimate trade show manager.

Part 1 - Getting Started: Trade Show Basics

1

Checklist for a Successful Trade Show

It's Monday morning and Bonnie is stuck in traffic, but she doesn't care. She doesn't care because she's going to have a great day. Sitting on the seat next to her is a report on last week's trade show. It glows. It practically floats.

The annual trade show was the industry's most important and glamorous event. And all of the company's competitors exhibit. Companies whose annual sales climb into the hundreds of millions of dollars were there, along with their customers – and so was Bonnie.

Over the course of the three-day event, a steady stream of people flowed through the exhibit. Most of them were looking for exactly the kind of products Bonnie's company was offering. Many of them expected to purchase within the next few months. In the end, the salespeople working in the exhibit booth managed to collect over 700 leads.

One person visiting the booth, commonly referred to as an attendee, was his company's chief decision-maker on a huge project. Bonnie's company's ace salesperson had tried for months to get in front of this man, with no success. The salesperson did a double take when she read the man's name tag. But she moved in quickly, and within a half an hour, the man asked her to bid on his project.

The attendees flocked around the new product being introduced at the show. This was a problem, because the one editor unable to attend the pre-show press conference couldn't get a good look at it when he stopped by just after the show opened. Fortunately, the crowd piqued his interest, so he made a point to drop back by the booth during a lull.

The press conference also went well. A couple of the editors mentioned that they planned to do a few feature stories on the new product. Another editor asked to interview the company's president.

Bonnie may be inching along the freeway now, but soon she will turn in her wonderful report. She will pass by the offices of salespeople hard at work, happily following up on leads and preparing bids. Then she will spend the rest of the morning returning the phone calls of editors who've called with follow up questions and requests for interviews.

A story with a happy ending? Absolutely. It can happen. You can write your own successful trade show story.

It is Monday morning, you're about to hand in your post show report. What does it say?

Checklist for a Successful Trade Show

So, how do you get there from here? How do you get from "Hey, lets do a trade show!" to a fist full of leads? Thousands of companies successfully exhibit at trade shows every year, boosting sales and enhancing their image in the process. So can you.

The path to trade show success looks a lot like a jumbled maze. But there is one thing that every successful trade show manager does. They turn the maze into a checklist for success.

Know Your Goals

Let's say you decide that you want to buy a car. That's a goal. So off you go to the nearest dealership. A salesman approaches and strikes up a conversation. An hour later, you are filling out loan paperwork for a red Mustang convertible. It's expensive. But by now, you really need that convertible, and hey, you deserve it. Is this how you go about buying a new car? No, it's probably not.

By the time you walk into the dealership, you've probably decided *why* you need or want a new car, the model and how much you are willing to pay. You've probably saved up the down payment, and planned an affordable monthly car payment.

In other words, you decided that you wanted to buy a new car. You set up specific goals that allow you to make the purchase. If you don't set specific goals, you won't be able to plot a specific course, and you won't get that car.

Trade show planning works the same way. If you don't set specific goals, you risk wasting money you can't afford to spend. If your aren't defined, you have no way of measuring your success. Let's look at the four most common goals of trade show exhibitors.

Leads. All exhibitors want to end up with a fist full of leads. But if all an exhibitor wants is lots of leads, then she is better off simply renting the list of attendees and skipping the trade show. What exhibitors really want is a fist full of highly-qualified leads. In three weeks or three months time, a certain percentage of these leads will turn into closed deals.

Here are some factors to consider, when generating leads is a priority:

- How many leads do you want?
- How many salespeople do you need at the show to capture these leads?
- How much time do your salespeople need qualify an attendee?
- How many hours will the trade show floor be open?
- What percentage of these leads do you expect to turn into sales?
- What is the average dollar-amount of these sales?
- What is the turnaround time, from opening to closing, of the average sale?
- What is the batting average of each salesperson? What percentage of leads is she or he able to turn into sales?

Answering these questions will help you plan your exhibit, from the number of salespeople staffing the exhibit booth, the types of questions they will use to qualify an attendee as a lead, to the size of the exhibit itself.

Say for example, you want to generate 500 leads from a particular trade show. You already know that the show floor is open to attendees for a total of 30 hours. It takes your salespeople about 10 minutes to qualify an attendee as a lead – close six leads per hour, per salesperson. How many salespeople do you need to staff the booth?

1 salesperson x 6 leads/hour x 30 hours = 180 leads/salesperson

1 salesperson/180 leads x 500 leads = 2.8 salespeople

You will need at least three salespeople staffing the exhibit booth at all times. Remember to take into account lunch breaks for the staff. The exhibit booth staff must be able to quickly draw likely candidates into the booth and qualify them with great diplomacy.

Corporate Image. Enhancing the company's image is an underlying concern in any trade show. Whether intentional or not, your exhibit creates a certain picture of your company. If red and black colors and angular shapes dominate your exhibit design, you are telling people that your company is aggressive. If your exhibit resembles a 1950s diner, people will peg your company as hip and creative.

You can use the trade show to create a specific public awareness of your company, which you tailor according to your own plan. If changing, updating or publicizing your company's image is a major goal of the trade show, you will be working closely with your marketing plan and your PR department or agency. Updating or changing corporate image extends beyond the scope of a trade show.

Here are some reasons why you may want to focus on your corporate image:

• Differentiate your company from your competitors.
• Associate certain qualities or values with your company.
• Update your company's image or logo.

•Introduce a new corporate logo.

•Overcome a negative corporate image.

Introduce a new product line. Trade shows are a great place to introduce a new product line. Especially if it is a departure from your traditional offerings. Here, you have access to qualified buyers and trade press, all under one roof. Your exhibit becomes a launch pad where you can show off the new product.

The tools for launching a new product at a trade show are endless. In-booth presentations range from simple slide show-style affairs to full scale theatrical productions. With some pre-show planning, you can hold a press conference before the event opens. This is an inexpensive and highly useful way of getting your new product and your company in the news.

Meet your customers. Bringing in new customers is all well and good. A certain percentage of your business *should* be new accounts. However, it is an expensive venture. And though the urge can be overwhelming to focus solely on acquiring new accounts, this kind of tunnel vision is deadly. Long-term customer relationships are vital to a company's long term success.

As any experienced salesperson will tell you, nothing beats quality face time with the customers. Companies use trade shows to hook up with faithful customers, to say, "thanks for your business", to solidify relationships.

If meeting your existing customers is one of your chief goals, you should consider renting a hospitality suite in a hotel convenient to the convention center. If meeting your existing customers is your *only* goal, you might not need to exhibit at all.

Here are some other ways to meet your customers.

•Rent a hospitality suite and make appointments to meet your customers.

•Throw an invitation-only cocktail party, lunch or brunch for your customers.

•Sponsor a table at a lunch, brunch or dinner given by trade show management.

•Host a special event organized by trade show management.

•Invite customers to your exhibit for a meeting or private product demonstration.

Train Your Sales Staff

Picture this: Alpha, Inc. just exhibited in the industry's biggest trade show. Attendance was at an all-time high. Over 100,000 corporate officers, decision makers and decision influencers attended an event that could result in millions of dollars in sales for successful exhibitors.

AI's marketing manager planned the event a year in advance. She worked and toiled. She won the cooperation of the various departments in the company who contribute to the trade show effort. The exhibit was perfect-economical yet attractive. It conveyed the company's image as an up-and-coming manufacturer of medical instruments. The new product demonstration was clever, and consistently drew crowds.

AI's goal was to collect at least 500 highly qualified leads, but they ended up with less than 80. Or worse, they got the 500 little slips of paper, but after weeks of follow up, they found that only a few leads turned into sales. Very small sales, at that – because AI's booth staff tried to qualify anyone and everyone who walked through the exhibit. In other words, AI's booth staff didn't really qualify anyone.

The point is AI spent a lot of money to exhibit at the trade show, and came home with only two workable leads. Luke-warm leads, at that. A goal of 500 leads is great. But 500 highly qualified leads is better.

You can have just the right booth space, in a perfect location, lots of foot traffic and the perfect number of salespeople staffing the booth. But unless those salespeople can do three things well, 498 of the leads are little slips of worthless paper:

Hook 'em. The salesperson stands next to one of the exhibit's displays. A couple of attendees approach, obviously interested in the product being featured. One of the attendees turns to the salesperson and asks her to tell him more about the product.

It'd be great if it was always this easy. You'd think that everyone interested in a certain type of product would seek out every display related to his or her needs. They'd swap business cards. But it rarely happens.

A great salesperson doesn't wait for a potential lead to approach her. In fact, she doesn't wait for them to move into her space. She watches. She reads name tags. She notices what they look like, what they are looking at. She sizes them up and casually approaches. She doesn't pounce; she's relaxed. She starts a conversation.

A great salesperson takes control of the exchange before it even starts. She pre-qualifies the lead, staying one step ahead of the game. Because she minimizes the time she spends with low quality leads, she ends up with more high quality leads that are more likely to result in a sale.

Reel 'em in. Regardless of who approaches whom, a great salesperson keeps the conversation light, friendly and professional. She knows that her goal is to qualify or disqualify the attendee quickly and move on to the next one. How does she do this? She has a certain process, one that she has memorized and practiced.

- Always make sure the attendee ends up believing that the company is great, the salesperson is great, and the products are great.
- Find out who the attendee is, who he works for and what position he holds with his company.
- Find out what types of products and services he is interested in.
- Find out if and when he plans to purchase, and how much he plans to spend.
- If there is a fit between the companies, put the attendee in front of the product display that most closely matches his requirements.
- Record the attendee's name, company, address, and any other follow-up information.

The successful salesperson works from a script. A script that she improvises and alters to fit the situation. It has a beginning, a middle and an end – and a running time.

Anyone attending a trade show knows that a great salesperson's only reason for talking to him or her is to find out if they might make a good sales lead. But they don't like to think someone is holding them by the ankle, shaking the loose change out of their pockets. The salesperson makes it a smooth experience for the attendee.

Close them. The salesperson has an agenda: Generate a maximum number of leads by the end of the show. To do this, she must regulate the amount of time she spends with each attendee. At the appropriate moment, she ends the conversation. This might be when she has qualified the lead, captured the information and promised to follow up. Often it is when she has determined that the attendee does not qualify as a sales lead.

In either case, the great salesperson closes the conversation with great diplomacy. She is polite and professional, and never ever abrupt. The attendee leaves with the best possible impression of the company, its products, and the salesperson's professionalism. She does this whether or not the attendee is a qualified sales lead.

Interdepartmental Cooperation

The perfect trade show. All of your materials made it to the convention center. The exhibit went up with a minimum of problems. Everything looked great, the demonstration equipment performed flawlessly and the booth staff did a wonderful job collecting leads.

If you are like most trade show managers, you rely heavily on the cooperation of people outside your own staff. In fact, you may not even *have* a staff. Trade show management is probably just one aspect of your job. You may be the marketing manager with one or two staff members, or you may have no staff at all. You might be a sales director, charged with coordinating all of the marketing events for your division. You may even be the account executive for the company's PR agency, or the marketing consultant.

Whatever your position and however many staff you do or do not have, there is one absolute truth about making a successful trade show happen. *You must have the cooperation* of virtually *every department* in the company.

Some people are chosen to work on the trade show because they are the best at what they do. Some because they are the only person available, and some because they are the only people within the company who performs the specific job. One thing they all have in common: none of them volunteered.

Here are the people who make up your trade show team:

Upper management. You probably do all of the research, recommendations and basic footwork. But unless you are a vice president or director, someone else makes the final decisions. You may recommend the marketing budget, you may help design the marketing plan, but you probably don't have the final word. That is the Top Dog's job.

It is important to be subtle in soliciting cooperation from the Top Dog. The Top Dog is open to input from the lower ranks, he says. Even the mailroom guy can walk into his office and recommend a better way to run the company and he'll certainly listen. He says.

In reality Top Dogs want to hear things that reinforce their position as Top Dogs. They want recommendations – when they ask for them. They want options. They want information so that they can make top dog decisions.

So, give the Top Dog what he wants. Find out *his* goals for the company. Understand his goals. You'll be in a good position to recommend great trade shows. Don't tell the Top Dog that he *must* sign the contract 12 months in advance. Tell him that his best opportunity for getting a prime spot in the trade show is by signing 12 months in advance. Let *him* make the decision.

Accounts payable. The accounts payable manager is responsible for all sorts of invoices and bills associated with the company's business. Trade show related payables are much the same as the company's other bills.

However, there can be some subtle differences. The invoice for the advertisement in the trade show directory can look a lot like the one for advertisement in a regular trade magazine. If she's not careful, the accounts payable manager might assume the invoice is a duplicate, and delay payment.

Some trade shows do not send invoices for space rental contracts. Instead, they rely on the company to remember payment deadlines.

You can help the accounts payable manager by letting her know in advance about all the trade show related billables. Make sure each item has its own purchase order. And provide her with copies of all your paperwork. Going over the details with her will give her the opportunity to ask questions and let you build up rapport.

Purchasing department. Without the cooperation of the purchasing agent, your trade show boat will sink. From the space rental contract to the advertisements to the carpet rental to the extra business cards, everything needs a purchase order.

Life would be great if your company's purchasing agent threw purchase order numbers at you every time you asked. You'd have that laptop and fax machine for your home office – and the trip to Hawaii for that really important conference. But they don't. They like their jobs too much.

The purchasing agent must justify every expenditure. So he needs to know from you *why* you need extra business cards for certain staff members. And why you suddenly need another advertisement, when you already have one running. Explain why you need those purchase orders.

In addition to all the obvious trade show expenses, you may need to have some special give-away items produced. Pens and coffee mugs with the company logo and address, tee shirts, little solar powered calculators, tote bags. Perhaps you design them and specify the materials or you may find a company in New Jersey to make them for you. But it is the purchasing agent who finds the company in Taiwan who makes them for 40 percent less.

Production. A thousand of new computers come off the assembly line each week. But for the trade show, you want several different configurations to display. You need to demonstrate your company's broadest capabilities. The production manager must pull several people off the line to build your special configurations. If the line is already running at full capacity he doesn't have any production personnel to spare.

The new configurations are different, and not what the line is set up to produce. It can be a big expensive deal for the production manager to produce the products for your display equipment.

Whether your company sells computers or toys, the products you want to display at the trade show are often built-to-order items. You need to work closely with your production manager to be sure he can provide you with product displays.

If you buy your products from another company to resell under your own label, you need to allow extra time for that company to produce and deliver the items.

Product design engineers. The latest greatest computer modem, the video game to shut out the competition, the new doll that eats, walks and talks – in three different languages. You are introducing a new product at the trade show.

Two years before the show, it's a twinkle in the product manager's eye. A year before the show, the design is set. Six months before the show, it's being tested. Two months before the show it's being redesigned.

You are shipping the display products to the show and they are – working perfectly? Not working, but look as if they could? Working, but need an engineer to set them up and get them running? Any one of these scenarios can be handled. You just need to know ahead of time which one it is going to be.

Keep close tabs on the product design engineers' progress from beginning to end. Do it in a supportive, congenial way.

"How's the family… and by the way, have you figured out why the flux capacitor keeps burning out on the new 'Mr. Fusion' food processor?" As if you were making casual conversation. "No? Golly. How frustrating for you."

Nothing brings out an engineer's sense of cooperation more than a friendly conversation about a technical problem. Two colleagues, solving a puzzle. Nothing alienates an engineer more than, "What!? What's wrong? When will you figure it out?" Pressure, immediate answers and demands.

Technical services. It's Monday morning. The technical services manager is interviewing candidates to replace the second shift technician who quit last week. The interview are not going well. At least those two new guys she hired last month are training up nicely. It's been hectic since upper management decided to add weekend phone support. Well, *more* hectic.

She's looking at a full week. Everyone is on edge about the big contract proposal due this week. She's been busy helping the sales manager with special product configurations and now her own technical services module is late.

On top of that, the company's network upgrade has to be complete before the end of the month. With her lead technician covering staff vacations, she's been doing most of the work herself. Yes, she's even in charge of the company's computer network.

The marketing manager keeps asking when she'll have time to review a few trade show-related issues. She's been able to clear her schedule enough to be a part of the trade show set-up team, even the booth staff. But she's had to put off doing the certification testing for that new 'Mr. Fusion' thing until after the show.

She's your best friend. Your technical services team member can help calculate your electrical requirements for the display equipment and exhibit. She can help build and test display products for which the production line is unequipped. She can help set up the display equipment and exhibit at the trade show. She can be an effective member of the booth staff during the show.

The technical services team member is also the toughest draft pick. She is usually overworked and understaffed. With that in mind, there are five things you can do to help her cooperate with you:

1. Become a technical expert yourself.

2. Take on as much technical responsibility for display products, without overstepping your authority.

3. Give the technical services manager your trade show calendar well ahead of time.

4. Let her know what your needs will be, so that she can plug the show into her schedule.

5. Accommodate the technical services manager's schedule. It's not very flexible, and there isn't much she can do about it.

Office assistant. You have to put together 50 press kits, about an hour's worth of pulling and collating brochures, press releases and corporate backgrounders, placing them in presentation folders, inserting your business card and stapling slides to the flap.

There are pre-show mailers to send – print several hundred mailing labels, affix them to the mailer along with postage.

Mail out sales letters with invitations and guest passes. Print out the letters and labels. Stuff and seal the envelopes. Postage. Sales orders for display equipment. Dozens of little, time consuming tasks.

Because "trade show" is synonymous with "deadline", these time drains can be fatal. You have to change the press kit at the last minute. It has to ship via overnight express service. So it has to be reassembled and ready to go in less than an hour, because that's when the express office closes. You have to drive it there. You also have a final meeting to review the schedule with your staff.

You need an office assistant, and you need her now.

All of this, even working with tight deadlines, comes with the territory for office assistants. If she is not a regular part of your staff, then she's doing you a favor. Because she is a shared resource, she's under a lot of pressure. There are three things you can do to make helping you easier.

Avoid dumping tasks on her at the last minute. If you know those guest passes have to go out in two weeks, tell her now.

- Help *her* out.
- If she helps you with a last-minute emergency, repay the consideration.
- Maybe you need those press kits reassembled and delivered to the overnight express service in less than an hour. Help her with that important mailing, the one she's doing for one of her other bosses. The one she set aside to help you.
- Be very clear in telling her what you need done. Type it up along with the deadline and any information she needs to complete the task.

•One last thing - always use the same office assistant to help you with trade show work. She will develop a knowledge base that makes her more efficient.

Sales. The sales department needs fresh leads to boost their numbers. You need detailed information about their market segment.

Upper management wants to know if the cost of exhibiting is justified. So you need to know from the sales department how many of last year's trade show leads turned into sales. The sales manager wants to know why you are so curious about his business.

You need to know whether this is the right trade show for the company. The sales manager already knows he wants to break into the show's target market.

The relationship between sales and marketing is a mix of interdependence and caution. According to one viewpoint, the marketing department is an appendage of sales. Another viewpoint pegs the sales department as a component of the marketing effort.

No matter which way you look at it, these issues need to be addressed. The two entities rely on each other to get the job done.

The trade show or marketing manager is charged with:

•Making sure each trade show is in the company's best interest.

•Reporting to upper management the return on their trade show investment.

•Knowing and understand the company's target market.

•Making sure the booth staff is well trained.

•Doing everything possible to get attendees into the exhibit.

•Making sure the sales staff has everything they need to turn trade show leads into sales.

To do these things, she needs access to general information about the company's customers. She needs to:

•Confer with the sales manager. Know what his goals are.

•Hold planning meetings with the upper management, the sales manager and his staff.

•Have some oversight of the sales staff while they are working as booth staff.

•Get post-show lead management information, to assess the show's success.

If it sounds like an exchange of cooperation, it is. Here are three things you can do to maximize your success.

1. Understand what the sales manager's professional goals are. Maybe he sees himself as the future vice president of sales and marketing. Maybe he sees you as his competition. Let him know, or think, you are his ally.

2. Adapt your style of communication to his. If the sales manager is big on inter-office e-mail, use it. If he is a visual learner, say, "I see," a lot. If he's kinesthetic, "I feel." Good communication skills let you nudge him along, even manage *him*, without his knowing it.

3. Let him make as many decisions as possible, without giving up your authority. He can choose the booth personnel, make the staffing schedule and decide who bunks with whom at the hotel during the show. You can throw in a few decisions like, what airline he and his salespeople use to get to the show city. That's probably more important to him than it is to you.

Cheat Sheet

Now you have a good overview of what goes into managing a successful trade show. As the trade show manager, you may not be the chief decision maker. You may not be a manager. You may be the marketing manager, marketing assistant or sales manager. In fact the company may not employ you at all. You may work for the company's PR or marketing firm.

The best way to manage trade shows is to charge one person with responsibility for the entire project. Trade show management draws on a variety of skills. As the trade show manager, whatever position you hold, you must be able to manage bosses and colleagues. You must understand principles of artistic design. You must understand the technology behind the company's product or services.

Here's what else you've learned so far:

•Know your goals—see chapter 2.

•Interdepartmental cooperation—right here in chapter 1.

2

Planning: The Best Foundation

Planning. You know the routine. It's the end of the year. Time to roll up your sleeves. Time to set new goals and plan new ploys. Maybe sales were a little flat last year. Maybe it's time to take the company to a new level. Or maybe the director of sales heard about a great trade show. It's a perfect way to introduce the new product line and reel in tons of luscious new prospects. Your boss calls you into her office and tells you, "We need to do some trade shows next year."

So you trudge back to your office. Your boss mentioned Spring Comdex and PC Expo – two famous business-to-business computer trade shows. The director of sales wants to launch his new product line at the National Association of Broadcaster's (NAB) cornerstone event.

You scramble to gather information on all three shows. A few hours later you've found out that Spring Comdex, a mid-April show has a few spaces still available, but only one of them is in a workable location.

NAB, held in Las Vegas, will take place in March, less than four months away. The sales representative was polite enough not to laugh at you. But just barely. She places you on a waiting list for a

100 square foot space in a dark corner. NAB is a very popular trade show and the prime booth locations sold out several months ago.

PC Expo has several prime spaces available. It is held in June – in New York City. It's much more expensive than NAB and appeals to a broader market. But it's a well-known show held in one of the most accessible cities in the world. So it must be a good show, right?

It might be. It might not be. The trouble is, at this point you don't really know. You don't know if the show targets your specific market, or if its audience contains the right mix of decision-makers. You don't know the show's track record. More importantly, you don't know how much you will eventually spend on this show, or whether you'll be able to generate enough sales to justify the cost.

Does this scene sound familiar? If you work for a start-up, or a small or medium sized business, it probably does. Planning a trade show isn't brain surgery, but it is a process requiring many steps. And the first step starts at least one year before the event. So, if you are considering a trade show in March of 2003, then you need to begin planning no later than March of 2002.

Plotting Your Course a Year in Advance

Ms. Boss and Mr. Director of Sales may think that they are ahead of the game. After all, the marketing hype won't hit the industry publications for another two or three months, right? But waiting to plan a trade show schedule until the event shows up on the bosses' radar is disastrous. Here is what you need to know in order to keep your company – and yourself out of trouble.

All of the larger shows start renting spaces a year prior to the show date. In fact, they start renting spaces for the Expo 2003 event during Expo 2002. Moreover, some of the more popular shows sell out their best spaces in only a few weeks. The National Association of Broadcasters, who hold their main event at the Las Vegas Convention Center and the Las Vegas Hilton *during* the Spring, rent out all of their space in the Convention Center, and most of the space at the Hilton during the show one year prior.

Another consideration is *priority points*. Larger shows use a reward system to keep exhibitors returning year after year. Here is how it works: Exhibitors sign up for next year's event at meetings that are arranged in advance by show management. During your meeting, you are offered whatever space remains. The earlier your appointment for this meeting, the better your selections.

The number of priority points you accumulate determines your appointment time. Show management awards priority points based on the number of consecutive events at which you have exhibited. The more consecutive years, the more priority points. Show management also considers the size of the space you've rented in the previous year – the larger the space, the more priority points.

Very small shows do not use the priority point system and usually make the floor plan available three to six months before the event.

But there is a hidden danger in renting space far in advance of the show. Scheduling conflicts. If you only have one exhibit and not enough in the budget to rent a second one, be careful not to sign up for concurrent shows.

Also, remember that it takes a certain amount of time to ship property from one convention center to another. Until scientists perfect the teleportation device, allow at least one week between shows. You need to sit down with a calendar, a map and an idea of your resources when putting together your schedule.

Selecting Shows in Which to Exhibit

Each year thousands of trade shows of all shapes and sizes provide a forum for companies and their customers to meet face to face. If you've been working in your industry for any length of time, you've come across at least one or two. There are dozens, perhaps hundreds more. So, how do you extend your list? Where do you find shows? How do you decide which ones to exhibit in?

Why Show It

The very first step in planning a trade show search is to determine your goals. What do you expect to get from exhibiting in a trade show? This is such an obvious step that many neglect to establish clear objectives.

Exhibiting at a trade show without a clear picture of your expectations is like buying a car without knowing what you really want. We all have a pretty good idea of what we are looking for before we go shopping. We may want a car that makes us appear attractive to the opposite sex. We may want a car that is reliable, or economical, or safe.

We must be honest about what we want before we enter the dealership. If we don't, we may end up with a Volvo station wagon instead of the red Mustang convertible we secretly long for.

So, grab a pen and paper, or keyboard if you prefer, a copy of your company's marketing plan and record exactly what you expect your company to gain from exhibiting. Be sure to take into consideration the hopes and dreams of that sales director, too.

Here are some excellent reasons to exhibit at a trade show:
•Enhance, change or introduce the corporate image.
•Introduce a new product.
•Meet new prospects.
•Connect with existing customers.
•Close some direct sales – set a certain number of sales and a certain dollar amount for each sale.
•Generate a specific number of leads.
•Generate a specific number of leads for your distributors.

Who to Show It To

Who are your customers? Who do you want to reach at the trade show? Do you sell your product to other businesses? Or do you sell it to Joan Q. Public? Perhaps your product is a mass consumer item such as a personal computer or an automatic dishwasher, but you sell it through a channel rather than directly to the consumer. If this is the case, than you may want to exhibit at a business-to-business rather than a mass consumer event.

Armed with a list of your goals and audience, you are ready to find the perfect show or shows. You may already know of a few candidates. Gathering information is easy. If you've heard of it, it has a web site. Simply point your web browser to one of the popular search engines, perform a search on the show and watch the web address pop up.

More Trade Shows

A great way to fill out a list of shows worth considering is to see where your competitors are exhibiting. Another resource is companies within your market. If you sell computer servers, find out where the major manufacturer of networking peripherals is exhibiting. Many companies post their trade show schedules on their web pages.

Magazines sponsor many trade shows. Contact the magazine for their lists or visit their web site. If you are really serious about generating a large list of possible shows, visit the web site of the magazine's parent publisher. You will find a smorgasbord of magazines to research.

Convention centers post lists of events on their web sites as well. Virtually every major city has a convention center.

Another great resource is the market leader in your industry. Very large corporations whose product serves as a platform for products of other companies in the industry will often host events that showcase their own products along with those of their partners.

Microsoft operating systems and office suites serve as platforms for many business and personal hardware products. This industry leader produces and hosts a number of symbiotic events to showcase companies selling products that depend on Microsoft software. In helping corporate partners reach their customers, Microsoft hopes to boost sales of their own products.

Other obvious resources are trade associations and special interest organizations. The National Association of Broadcasters, for example, produces several large events. Appendix A provides an expanded set of resources.

Should You or Shouldn't You

Mirror, mirror on the wall, which trade show is the fairest of them all? Wouldn't it be great if a wise face appeared and just forked over the list? Of course, a magic mirror would also have the winning numbers for tomorrow's $35 million lottery…so why bother about trade shows? Because trade shows can bring us sales!

The fairest shows are the ones that deliver the right audience, in copious numbers, for the most reasonable cost. That's delivery, audience, numbers and cost. Instead of a magic mirror, look to the show's marketing kit.

All major shows and most small and regional shows make their promotional material available through their web site. You can ask a sales representative to mail a kit, but it is much quicker to download the kit in electronic format or to print the web page.

The show's marketing kit includes detailed information on its target market and attendee profiles. The kit should be able to show you what percentage of attendees are expected to be buyers, what percentage are specifiers, corporate heads and decision makers. It may also tell you probable budgets of attendees, and details about when and how much they intend to buy.

Many marketing kits include facts and figures from the previous year's event along with comments from high profile attendees and exhibitors. But don't take the marketing kit at face value. It is a sales tool for the people who own the show, not a public service announcement. Spend a little more time digging for information before making a decision on whether or not to exhibit at a show. Ask colleagues at other companies in your industry about their experiences with the show. Pay attention to the industry buzz and news coverage of last year's event.

Here's another tip: Find out how well the show's owners promote the event. Take a look at last year's exhibitor's manual or exhibitor's marketing kit and examine the marketing and promotional opportunities available to exhibitors. If you cannot get your hands on last year's kit, take a look at the show's web site. You may be able to gain access to the section designed for exhibitors, which contains much of the same information. And while you're there, consider how well the web site itself promotes the event. If you think they do a poor job of attracting their target audience, then chances are they are doing a poor job of marketing their event.

What is the quality of the marketing kit itself? If the kit is well organized and easy to use, then chances are the show is well organized. If the kit is attractively designed with well-integrated graphical elements, then chances are the show will be well marketed.

Tools of the Trade

The handiest tool for planning your trade show calendar is a nice yearly planner. Quarterly planners also work. You will need to be able to write on them. A yearly calendar lets you see the entire year at a glance, which is especially important if you are exhibiting in several shows.

Research

In planning your trade show schedule, the first step is to research and find a show or shows in which you want to exhibit and which will bring you a maximum return on your investment. There are several criteria to consider when choosing a show. There are also a few pitfalls to watch out for. Selecting shows is covered later in this chapter. Appendix A lists several great places for finding shows in which to exhibit.

Timing is Everything

All major shows and most regional shows publish their calendar 12 months prior to the event. They are always held during the same month each year, during the same days of the week. Fall Comdex is always in November, NAB is always held in March and PC Expo is always held in June. However, the week of the month may change. You may be able to find out the official dates before the 12-month window by contacting your sales representative for the show.

If you are sitting down in January of 2002 to plan your 2003 calendar, keep in mind that, though you can estimate show dates with a lot of confidence, you may still need to make changes later on.

Got Booth?

Next, you need to know how much booth property you have available. Does your company currently own a booth? If so, does it need refurbishing? You need to know its current condition. If it needs refurbishing, you must get an estimate on how much time the work will take and find an appropriate time during the year to have the work done. Refurbishing can take anywhere from one to six weeks. Extensive artwork or an elaborate exhibit requires even more time.

Also keep in mind that booth repair and building is sometimes a seasonal service. Many trade shows, especially business-to-business events occur during the spring and fall. It follows that booth manufacturers have busy seasons during these times as well.

Some questions to ask yourself: Will you have the budget to rent a property in order to exhibit at simultaneous or closely scheduled shows, should the need arise? Will you be able to supply the demonstration equipment?

Populating the Property

You also need to know how many people are available to work at the show(s). Calculate the number of salespeople based on the size of the space and the number of days of the show.

Consider which of your candidates are best qualified to work at the trade show. Trade show sales uses a different set of talent than other forms of selling. Also consider that while sales personnel are working the show, they are not in the office or in the field servicing existing accounts.

What technical and set-up staff will you need at the show?

Having at least a rough idea of your booth staff helps you avoid conflicts with personal work schedules.

Selecting a Great Space

You've found the show and you have the marketing kit, so you have a copy of the space rental contract. You know how much each square foot is going to cost and you are ready to select a great space. This is not a difficult process, but break out your ballet slippers, because it *is* a delicate dance.

A Matter of Size

What size space do you want to rent? Smaller shows provide a minimum booth size of eight feet by 10 feet. That's eight feet deep (from the front of the booth to the rear) and 10 feet wide, increasing in 10-foot wide increments. If the trade show is held in a hotel's or small city's convention facility, most booths will be eight feet deep.

Booths at larger venues start at 10 foot by 10 foot (100 square feet) and increase in 10 square foot increments. 10 x 20 (200 square feet, 20 x 20 (400 square feet), 40 x 50 (2,000 square feet) and more .You may already be limited by the size of your booth property or budget. Or you may be flexible.

If you already own an exhibit property, find out what size or sizes it can be configured to. How much space does your booth property occupy, and how much space is left for sales staff and attendees? The perfect exhibit takes up no more than 30 percent of the booth space, leaving 70 percent for salespeople and attendees.

How many leads you would like to walk away with at the end of the show? The number of leads you "capture" at a show are the product of total show hours and number of booth staff. How many salespeople do you have available to work the booth? How many leads can you expect your sales staff to generate in a given period of time? A good salesperson can turn a lead in about 10 minutes, working out to about six leads per hour.

Each salesperson needs about 25 square feet of open space in which to work. If you want 500 leads from a show, and that show runs for 21 hours (seven hours a day for three days), you need two or three salespeople working the booth at all times. If your property occupies 25 square feet, three salespeople will fit comfortably into the remaining 75 square feet of a 100 square foot space.

Remember to account for meal breaks. A reasonable cast for the hypothetical show is four salespeople. That fourth person fills in during lunch and dinner.

Now that you know what size you are looking for, you are ready to select a space. The trade show's floor plan is always included in the marketing kit, but you should ask your sales representative to provide you with a copy of the most current plan. Have her mark the available spaces in your size and price range. You should also ask her for a list of current exhibitors and their booth assignments. This will help you select a space away from companies you want to avoid, and near those with whom you want to align.

More Than Just Size

Of course, size *is* important. But you have another great feature to consider. How many sides of the booth space are open to the aisles? The greater your access to the aisles, the easier it is for attendees to flow into your exhibit. There are several types of exhibit space configurations to choose from.

In-line. These are spaces arranged in continuous line along an aisle and are limited to smaller exhibits. In-lines have one side open to the aisle. They are always eight-foot or 10-foot deep booths, and can be 10, 20, 30 feet or more in length. Usually though, an in-line is 10 or 20 feet wide.

Corner booth. The booth at the end of a series of in-line spaces exposes the exhibit to two aisles.

Peninsular or end cap. Exposed to aisles on three sides, a peninsular exhibit shares a side with one other exhibit. Peninsular spaces are usually in the range of 200 to 400 square feet.

Island. An island space exposes the exhibit to all four aisles – the most desirable arrangement. Islands are rarely as small as 200 square feet and can range up into the thousands of square footage.

Location, Location, Location

In selecting a space, location is everything. There there are important keys to consider.

Your neighbors. You might want to avoid being near your competitors in order to set your company apart. Or, you might want to be placed near your competitors so that you can lure away their customers. You might want to be near the giants in your industry. If you sell computer hardware, selecting a space near the manufacturer of the most popular software will put you within reach of pre-qualified customers for your product.

The entrance. The closer you are to the entrance, the more attendees see your exhibit. It's simple. Attendees are saturated with all the excitement and presentations as they make their way from the entrance to the far reaches of the convention center floor. Or they just poop out. So a space near the entrance, along the one or two main aisles perpendicular to the entrance is the most desirable spot. They are also the most popular amongst exhibitors, and so sell out quickly.

Stages. Many of the larger shows offer platforms for presentations, demonstrations, speeches or even performances on the show floor. Bill Gates might offer a speech on the future of operating systems and the Internet, or an IBM executive might discuss latest developments in mass storage technology. If you select a space near one of these stages, you are exposed to a large group of motivated attendees.

Pavilions. During recent years, trade shows have begun setting aside floor space for market segments within the audience's industry. Pavilions are designed to provide you with a stream of motivated attendees with great interest in a particular type of product. Show designers do this by clustering exhibitors whose products appeals to a focused market.

For example, the computer trade show PC Expo includes an Internet pavilion in the floor plan. If your company is an Internet service provider, you will want to rent a space here. Your neighbors will be other Internet service providers, companies who develop software that makes it easier for people to access the Internet, modem manufacturers and consulting service providers, among others.

Look Out!

Now you know what to look for in a great booth space. Here are some things to look *out* for.

Bathrooms and snack bars. Some exhibitors intentionally locate themselves near the facilities—Not to coddle the booth staff, but because they believe it will increase the number of their leads. While it is true that most attendees visit these facilities least once, it is also true that their focus will *not* be on your exhibit.

The convention center itself. Before making your selection, you need to examine the floor plan carefully. Look for structural details of the exhibit hall that may affect your exhibit. Be aware of any weight-bearing columns located around your booth space. A column that is placed squarely in front of your exhibit can spoil your presentation.

Also be sure you know the height of the ceiling above your space. Don't assume that the height is the usual 18 feet throughout the convention center. One exhibitor who did not check ended up with a 12-foot clearance for her 12-foot exhibit. A tight fit, with no room for a hanging sign.

The hall within the hall. Many of the larger trade shows use more than one hall within a convention center. In addition to the main hall, a smaller hall or room houses the rest of the event. There are more available prime spaces in the smaller hall, making it seem like an attractive option. But in reality it is not, because fewer attendees make the effort to walk through the smaller hall.

Signing the Contract

You've selected your space and now all you have to do is sign the contract. Signing your name is a simple enough matter. But you need to make sure you read and understand all the fine print. The two most important things you need to know are the payment schedule and the terms for cancellation. If you are not the top decision-maker in your company, you need to make sure that the person who *does* decide understands the payment schedule and cancellation terms.

Most events require a down payment at the time you sign the contract, usually 25 percent of the contract amount. The remainder of the payments is made in quarterly installments. Most contracts do not allow for a refund, if at a later date, you change your mind about exhibiting.

But don't let that deter you from attempting a negotiation for cancellation, should you need to pull out of a show. The show's sponsor may own another show in which you want to exhibit. They might allow you to apply your payments from one to the other.

Beware! Some trade shows will hold you responsible for the entire contract amount if you cancel after a certain date. *Moreover, you will lose whatever seniority in space selection you've accrued.* So, if there is any chance at all that you might want to cancel your company's participation in the show, be very sure you understand show management's policy.

Some shows send an invoice for each payment. If the invoice is to go directly to your accounts payable department, make sure you've provided the department with a copy of the contract and the proper purchase order. Some shows do not send invoices, but rely on you to remember to send payments on time. It is up to you to make sure your accounts payable department has a copy of the contract, the payment schedule and all the internal documentation necessary to make payments.

The 12-Month Countdown!

If you wrote out all the action items involved in managing a successful trade show and laid them end-to-end, you'd have a task stretching from your desk to the moon. Taken individually, they look quite small. Fill out a form, write a press release, make some posters. Leave them until the last minute, and you're looking at a rough ride – without the space suit!

Yet that is what some companies do. It's not that they ignore the trade show, waiting until the last four or five weeks before the event to start planning. What happens is that the big cheese, the head of sales and marketing or the division sales manager enters the show dates into their calendar. Each month, they flip ahead in their calendar, making plans, setting goals. 11 months later, up pops the trade show.

Now the show is a priority. People rush around trying to get it all done in time for the launch. Panic ensues. Corners are cut. They may be able to launch it, but it still crashes and burns. If it can happen to NASA, it can happen to you.

A trade show is more than just those three days at the end of the month, 12 months from now. It is dozens of smaller events, each with their own deadlines. Many are interdisciplinary and must be integrated into existing marketing programs. Many just plain cost your company a lot of money if you leave them until a month before the show.

We'll get into more detailed planning in a later chapter. The following is a basic guideline. Your own plan may vary according to your trade show schedule and your resources.

12 Months Out – Planning to Plan

In the beginning *is research and planning.* A company's trade show schedule is only one part of its marketing program. Begin planning now, in order to integrate the show into the larger marketing plan.
- Research and select the show in which to exhibit.
- Select the space.
- Read the contract very carefully. Make sure you understand the terms for payment.
- Sign the contract and send it in with the first payment.
- Start planning the show.
- Start planning the budget.

11 Months Out – Precision Planning

Now is the time for all good plans to come together. All trade shows share common steps to success. Whether large or small, every show involves exhibit and demonstration planning, public relations, advertising, contracting for on-site services, shipping, travel arrangements, and dozens more. By generating a detailed schedule with starting dates and deadlines for each action item now, you avoid much heartache and panic later.

Several action items such as lead retrieval" , electrical and telecommunications services have deadlines imposed by the service provider. You won't know the official deadlines for these items until two or three months prior to the show. But it is easy to estimate deadlines for each of these. Deadlines for services are basically the same every year for a given show. For example, the deadline for "early bird discounts" for electrical and telecommunications is almost always three weeks prior to the show opening. The service providers will happily give you information on their individual policies.

- •Start planning a detailed schedule.
- •Start planning your objectives.

10 Months Out – The Exhibit

It's a small, small world. A trade show is like Disneyland. It is an exciting, glamorous little world, collected beneath a single roof. Each exhibit is an attraction, designed and built to entice you into its space. It can be as simple as a few tables and signs. Or it can be highly elaborate, with a two-story platform, meeting rooms and hourly product demonstrations.

What you need to decide is whether you want to own your own exhibit property, or rent someone else's. Designing and building your own exhibit property is an elaborate undertaking.

- •Start planning the exhibit.
- •If you do not already own one, you will need to decide whether you want to own or rent.
- •If you plan to have a custom exhibit designed and built for you, start researching and interviewing exhibit builders.

6 Months Out – Marketing

One For the Money. It's time now to begin designing the individual campaigns that will get your company and your exhibit noticed. All of these campaigns share the same creative resources. Starting now ensures that you will get it all done.

- Finalize show objectives.
- Start designing custom exhibit.
- Check on company literature to be handed out at the show.
- If you are planning a redesign or major updates, you should begin updating now.
- Start planning pre-show advertising, PR and direct mail.

4 Months Out – Getting Down to Business

Two for the Show. The exhibitor's manual arrives about two or three months before the show. However, you will receive a few forms in advance of the kit's arrival.

- Fill out and send in your request form for free complimentary guest passes as soon as they become available since delivery may take a month or more.
- Select service vendors for shipping and installation/dismantle.
- Review the exhibitor's manual as soon as it arrives.
- Finalize the exhibit design.
- Plan your hanging sign, if needed.
- Select the products you will display.
- Develop the floor plan for your exhibit.
- Select the booth staff.
- Make travel and hotel reservations.
- Begin pre-show advertising, PR and direct mail.
- Plan in-booth give-aways. Allow a few weeks for design, and up to several months for production.

3 Months Out – Production

Three to Get Ready. Three months may seem like a lot of time, but this is actually a critical point. Many creative and marketing decisions are being made. It is important for everyone involved –

from sales managers to upper management, even technical staff – to focus on creating a successful event.

- Be sure to review the exhibitor's manual.
- Plug in the deadline dates for all tasks related to the exhibitor's manual. Especially important are move-in dates and "early bird special" deadlines.
- Plan your in-booth demonstration or presentations.
- Send in your show guide listing.
- Plan your show guide advertisement.
- Start designing and producing your direct mail pieces.
- Send in authorization form, if you are using an exhibitor appointed contractor.
- Start designing and producing any required booth graphics or signage.

2 Months Out – Almost Crunch Time

Now you're cooking. The last two months before a trade show are naturally the most active. Timing is critical. You are managing a variety of outside vendors and company resources to complete whatever is necessary for your company to have a great trade show.

If the company that is building your exhibit is having trouble completing the work, you have a potentially serious problem. If the product you were planning to introduce at the show is hitting a design snag, that is another problem. Be sure to keep constant tabs on all on-going projects, and allow a few extra days for each one of them.

- Finish fabrication of your new exhibit.
- Set up the new exhibit for inspection. If it is an older exhibit, inspect for damage. If it is a new exhibit, give your booth staff the opportunity to bond with it.
- Finalize the company literature.
- Plan and prepare the press kits.
- Set up meetings between top company officials and editors, to hopefully gain some post show press coverage.

•Verify airline and hotel reservations. Plug the details into your planning document.

•Plan the sales training for your booth staff.

•Order the lead retrieval system.

•Fill out and send in the order form requesting labor to install your hanging sign.

•Fill out and send in the order forms and payments for your remaining services – telephone, electrical, water, and so forth.

•Reserve your van line or trucking company.

•Order and prepare your display products.

1 Month Out – Getting the Show on the Road

Down to the wire. Judging by the list below, the tasks seem simple enough. Just a lot of following up and packing. But nothing could be further from the truth. The last four weeks are where disasters are born. If you like emergencies, you'll love this month. If you're like the rest of us, be prepared to focus very carefully on follow-ups and preparation.

•Ship your hanging sign to the show site. The hanging sign is handled separately from the rest of your exhibit and must be shipped one to two weeks before of the rest of your exhibit.

•Confirm the receipt of all your service order forms and payments.

•Confirm the readiness of your exhibit, signage, collateral materials and press kit.

•Meet with booth staff to review final planning.

•Prepare the show-site office kit.

•Requisition the company credit card for on-site payments.

•Prepare the exhibit, demonstration equipment, press kits and gang box—tools ands supplies for set-up, for shipment.

•Ship all show equipment to arrive on the target move-in date.

•Prepare the exhibit file. This file should include copies of the original contract and all order forms.

•Distribute exhibitor badges, briefing packets and any training materials to the booth staff.

It's Show Time – Finally

Nerves of steel. That's what you will need. Despite all your careful preparation, things can and do go wrong. Be prepared to solve problems and calm frayed nerves. Dress comfortably and make sure you are well rested. Remember to breathe deeply.

•Verify the safe arrival of your shipment.
•Supervise set-up of the booth and the installation of any required services.
•Hold a pre-show meeting with booth staff prior to opening on the first day.
•Arrange for the sales leads to be e-mailed or shipped overnight to the home office.
•Contract for space in next year's show, if you plan on exhibiting.
•Supervise tear-down at the end of the show.

Cheat Sheet

Planning for most trade shows begins at least a year before the event. Trade show management is more complicated than ever before. From choosing the right shows, to getting the best space; even making sure you understand the space rental agreement. The trade show manager is responsible for pulling it all together.

The big "to-do" list is strewn out over a 12-month period. Unless your company participates in a lot of events, trade show management is not a full time job. Yet, even the simplest schedule will spin out of control if you do not plot the course a year in advance.

Here's what you learned in this chapter:

•Plan your trade show schedule a year in advance.
•Your resources and how to use them.
•How to select a great space.

•Reviewing and signing the contract.
•The 12-month countdown.

3
Getting and Staying Organized

The ideal company has a mission statement and business plan, and you better believe that making tons of money is a key part of that plan. There's a big pot of gold sitting at the end of the rainbow, and your company wants a big percentage of the profits. So the company has a marketing plan that describes how they are going to get there.

A good marketing plan is creative and adaptable. And it is specific. It states a goal. The company expects its annual sales will hit a certain number, which accounts for a specific share of the overall market.

The marketing plan lays out, in detail, what the company will do and what resources they will need to accomplish their goals. Advertising, public relations, direct mail and a web site are all key resources to reach specific marketing goals. So are trade shows.

Trade shows are not only subsets of the marketing plan, they use all of the same resources (advertising, public relations and so forth), plus a few more. Timing is as critical here as it is in any other marketing campaign. What's more, the trade show effort is interwoven with everything else. Advertisements serve a dual purpose, promoting the company image and announcing the trade show. Direct mail promoting the show has to follow the same style and tone as the rest of the company's literature.

Making sure the equipment is prepared and shipped on time is important. It is critical if you exhibit at several shows a year. From setting policy, to writing, designing, planning, managing, advertising, publicizing, setting up services, packing boxes, loading the truck and supervising set-up, you are responsible for dozens of trade-show related tasks. No matter how much of this you delegate, it's your responsibility to make sure it gets done. All of it.

The only way to stay ahead of this game is to get and stay organized. Getting organized is fun, if you are an accountant. Accountants have all sorts of tools to keep them on track, techniques and technology to keep the cash flow going. The whole field of accounting is based on organization.

Marketing, on the other hand, is based on creativity, analysis and persuasion. A marketing effort must be flexible. Yet it is just as goal oriented and driven by deadlines as any accounting program.

The Master "To Do" List

The first step in organizing a successful trade show is figuring out all of the other steps. Not to be flippant, but writing out a list of everything you need to do, no matter how minor, is the most important step of all. Everything goes on the list, delegated tasks, other people's jobs; if it relates to the trade show, it goes on the list. Because no matter who packs the equipment, builds the display products or writes the press release—one person is responsible for all of it. If you are reading this book, that person is probably you.

The basic steps are the same for every show. You may want to add a few your own to the list below.

Select a space. The show management sales representative will happily fax a copy of the floor map. Ask him to indicate all of the available spaces that are within your size range and budget.

Sign the space rental agreement. Obvious, right? But not so obvious that it can be omitted from the list. Most agreement contracts have the exhibitor write down their top three choices. If you coordinate with your sales representative, you can reserve the best available space. Be sure to fax a copy of the signed contract as soon as possible. Mail the original with a partial payment as soon as the check is ready. Keep several copies for your files.

Send in the guest pass order form. The guest pass order form is included in the exhibitor's manual, an information and form-filled binder provided by show management. The kit usually arrives one to three months before the show, but management often faxes or mails a few of these time-sensitive forms in advance. Fill out and fax this form as soon as you get it. The sooner you request your passes, the sooner you can mail them to your customers. For more information on this and other forms, please read **Chapter 7, Logistics**.

Exhibit description and product locator forms for the exhibit guide. These forms are also included in the exhibitor's manual. The information is used in the Exhibit Guide, which is handed to every attendee when they enter the show floor. If you delay these forms until the deadline, you will be able to include any last minute changes to your exhibit descriptions. Again, fax the completed form.

Exhibit description form for web site listing. Trade shows with this promotional opportunity typically send out or e-mail the form long before you receive the kit. It is in your best interest to fill it out and fax or transmit it early. The sooner you send it back, the sooner your listing is posted on the show's web site.

Exhibit description form for *Show Pre-View* and *Show Daily* publications. Your exhibit description may also appear in these special edition magazines or newspapers. Usually the publication picks up the information from your exhibit guide listing form, but not always.

Exhibitor badge order form. The form is included in the exhibitor's manual. Request these identification badges as soon as you know who within your organization will staff the booth. This is an easy one to amend, so be sure to make photocopies of the blank form. As more staffers are added to your list, simply fill out another form.

Exhibit guide advertisement insertion order form. Placing your advertisement in a premium position within the guide costs extra. Very extra. If you are not up to the higher cost but want a great position, send the insertion order as quickly as possible. The early bird gets a slight advantage.

Exhibit guide logo form. Having your logo printed next to the exhibit guide description is a nice, inexpensive way to call attention the company. Not all shows offer this opportunity, but those who do often include it on the insertion order form.

Show guide advertisement materials due. Unlike regular publications, the exhibit guide deadline is not flexible. If materials are due September 5th, then you'd better make sure your materials arrive on or before September 5th.

Exhibit guide logo due. Your logo is transmitted separately from your ad materials. Exhibit guide production staff may let you e-mail the logo in electronic format.

Begin exhibit guide advertisement design. Start with the end in mind. Plan backwards. If you want the materials by September 1st, and you know it takes four weeks to design an ad, then August 4th is your deadline for starting the ad.

Complete exhibit guide advertisement. Plan to have the completed ad in your hands at least a week before the deadline. You can over-night the package as late as one working day before the deadline. Those few extra days may come in handy. But be sure to consult a calendar. If September 5th falls on a Tuesday and you tell your graphic artist "I want it first thing Monday morning," you're in trouble. Monday is a public holiday.

Begin planning pre-show public relations campaign. The pre-show PR campaign may be as simple as sending out and supporting a single news release. Or it can be a complex operation. In either case, you need to sit down and make a plan with its own set of deadlines.

Plan the press kit. The press kit ships along with the exhibit and display equipment. Again, start with the end in mind. If you plan to ship on October 5th, you will begin packing and stacking October 3rd. Therefore, you want the press kits boxed and ready to go on October 3rd. Press kits have a standard format, and planning them is quite simple. But writing the news releases and backgrounders and making sure you have photographic slides takes time. Even if you have a PR agency handling these things for you, keep this item on your list.

Write the news release and corporate backgrounder. If you prepare your own press materials or hire a freelancer, allow two to three days to get the job done.

Order photographic slides for press kit. Allow three to five days for slide duplication. If you need to have new shots, call your photographer right away. Some book as far out as one month.

Prepare the press kit. This is a simple, labor intensive effort. If you are doing this in-house, allow about two hours to line up the materials and assemble the 50 to 100 folders.

Submit product for "Best of Show Award", if available. Not all shows give awards for great products, but many do. You'll probably need to fill out and send in a form to be considered. If show management does not send the form, you will need to call your sales representative—a few weeks before the show.

Prepare major signage: designed and produced. Chances are, you need new signs. Make a list of the different signs you will need. Do this no later than three months before the show. Depending on the complexity, design and production takes anywhere from one to four weeks. Remember that designers, photographers and "reprographic" service bureaus (the people who produce the sign) are busy, especially around trade show time.

Make travel arrangements. Make airline reservations at least two months before the show.

Make hotel reservations. The bigger the show, the earlier you need to make reservations. Make them at least one month prior. At least three, if the show is held in Las Vegas.

Make ground transportation arrangements. Reserve the car or van at the same time you make hotel arrangements.

Plan the new exhibit property. Planning and building a new exhibit is one of the most important items on your trade show "To Do" list. In fact, it is so important, an entire chapter, **4—How To**

Have a Great Booth and Graphics, is devoted to the subject. Fabricators are the outfits who design and build the exhibit.

Refurbish existing exhibit. Exhibits should be inspected for damage after each show. Refurbishing may take as little as one week or it can take as long as a month. Have your fabricator refurbish or repair the exhibit earlier rather than later. The fabricator may need to order materials from an out of state supplier. They may also have several other projects going on. Be sure to factor in these time constraints as well.

Plan the display products. The conventional wisdom is to plan the display products at least six months before the show. However, practical wisdom keeps a different schedule. Be as specific as you can, but keep your plan flexible. Start planning at least six months before the show, and adapt when necessary.

Produce the display products. Aim to have the completed products in your hands one week before you must ship to the show. Add a cushion of about ten percent to the production schedule. Remember to account for product tests, supply shortages and glitches in new products. The sales orders or other paperwork you painstakingly prepare will come in handy later, when you make out your shipping list.

Update and print collateral materials. Keeping brochures and product data sheets up to date is an ongoing job. Make sure that regular maintenance is scheduled with the show dates in mind. Aim to have the freshly printed material in your hands at least three weeks before the show.

Order the lead retrieval system. Most systems these days are electronic. Trade show management pre-selects a specific vendor. The vendor's order form is included in the exhibitor's manual. Some of the vendors have on-line ordering that lets you reserve and pay for your lead retrieval at their web site. You have several options available, starting from about $195. Take the time to read the descriptions and make a cost-effective selection. Order early and get an "early bird" discount. If you mail the form, make sure to include full payment, and give it enough time to reach its destination.

Order electrical service. Both the electrical and telecommunications order forms are due at the same time, and often to the same mailing address. The deadline is usually two to three weeks before the show. The form may look a little complicated at first, but once you become familiar with it, you are set for life. Many major convention centers use the same format.

The electrical service providers need to know your needs: how much power, how many outlets, and where to place outlets. To that end, they will ask you to provide a simple diagram of your planned exhibit. Mail the form along with full payment, to the address provided.

Order telecommunications service. These days, you have several options from which to choose. You can order a single line, several lines, one hand set with several lines, even a mobile phone. Some service providers include the hand set for free, others charge separately for the phone and the service. Whichever you choose, you'll be paying at least several hundred dollars. Mail the form along with full payment, to the address provided. Expect a phone bill a month or two after the show. Long distance calls by your booth staff are billed separately from the service rental.

Order installation and decoration (I&D). The designated exhibition service company at the trade show manages several related tasks. As a result, you will fill out several simple forms, make one payment and send them together to a single address. To verify orders, you only have to call one person.

Carpet and padding. There are two basic options for carpeting—basic and premium. The basic carpet is neat and clean. It is obviously basic, yet quite respectable. Premium carpet is thicker, and offers a wider variety of rich colors. But it is definitely more expensive. Padding is separate. Always order padding for basic carpet. Spend money, save feet. Padding can be added to premium carpet, but is not absolutely necessary.

Furniture. If you are bringing your own exhibit, you may not need to rent furniture. However, you will have a wide variety from which to choose.

Booth cleaning. It is the least expensive service, and well worth the price.

I&D Labor. Again, the convention center employs union labor to help you set up your exhibit. The form asks you how many workers you will need, how many hours and at what times you will need labor to set-up and tear-down your exhibit. Be aware that you are charged time-and-a-half for workers working after standard hours (eight a.m. to five p.m., weekdays, and weekends.) Avoid planning set-up or tear-down on public holidays. Labor, if they work on the holiday, costs double overtime.

Exhibitor Appointed Contractor *(EAC)*. You have the option of hiring an outside union contractor to set up your exhibit. They are a little bit more expensive, and well worth it. Outside contractors rely on repeat business and word-of-mouth advertising by happy customers. Their work must be of high a quality in order to maintain a good reputation.

Convention center labor, on the other hand, will always have repeat business, whether their work is good or bad. The convention center must be informed that you are choosing an EAC, with the EAC form.

Freight handling. The convention center employs union labor to receive the exhibitor's shipment and transport it to and from the exhibit floor. Handling is charged at a flat rate, per one hundred pounds. Estimate the weight of your entire shipment and fill out the form.

Shipping information. The convention center asks that you provide information about your shipment—the carrier, number of boxes and crates—so that they can schedule freight handling labor. There are no costs associated with this form.

Payment, credit card authorization and order recap. Enter estimated costs for services on the lines provided. Add the total and indicate your method of payment. Whether you pay by check or credit card, you must provide valid credit card information on this form. Make photocopies of each form before mailing the originals, with payment.

Plan the booth staff schedule. You already know who your booth staff will be. Now it's time to plan the work schedule.

Send in lights out request form. If, for some reason, you do not want the convention center lights above your space to shine, fill out this form and fax it in. Keep a copy for your files.

Schedule the shipment. Call your transportation company two to four weeks before you ship. Tell them when and where to pick up your exhibit and equipment. An early afternoon pickup gives you time to line everything up. While you're on the phone, make arrangements for the return shipment.

Prepare loose materials for shipment. "Loose materials" includes brochures, catalogues, product data sheets, small signs, press kits, office supplies and the gang box (set-up equipment). Inventory each box as you pack them. Plan to have them ready two days before you ship.

Prepare exhibit to ship. If you store the exhibit yourself, have it pulled out and delivered to the shipping department as near to the scheduled shipping time as possible. The best plan is to deliver it a few hours before the truck or van arrives. If your fabricator stores it, arrange ahead of time to have the exhibit ready to go. Make sure your truck or van line knows your schedule and any special delivery instructions.

Prepare display products to ship. Aim to have the products packed and ready to ship at least one or two days before the shipping date

Prepare shipment. If your shipping department has the room, begin assembling boxes and exhibit crates a day or two before shipping.

Ship. The day you choose to ship depends where you are shipping from, where you are shipping to, and when it needs to get there (target move in). Ask your trucking company or van line for time estimates, and schedule accordingly. Avoid your shipping department's busy days.

Targeted move in. Your exhibit equipment arrives at the convention center on your target move in day. Trade show management assigns dates based on the exhibitor's physical location on the show floor. Move in dates are listed in the exhibitor's manual.

Set-up. The big day arrives. Ideally, set-up begins at least one day after your targeted move in. This gives the freight handlers plenty of time to move your equipment into your space. Have your booth personnel check into their hotel a day before set-up, so that they are fresh and ready to work.

Show dates and hours. Show management publishes several months ahead, the days and hours the show floor is open.

Dismantle. Dismantle, or tear-down, begins as soon as the show closes on the last day. You have some choices here. You can begin dismantling your exhibit right away, or you can go back to the hotel, get some rest, and start bright and early the next morning. There are advantages and disadvantages to both, but most exhibitors start dismantling at the earliest opportunity.

Receive return materials. Your trucking company or van line delivers your equipment three days to one week after the show closes.

You may do things a little differently. But this is a basic master trade show "to do" list.

Start with the End in Mind—Setting Deadlines.

Cut off dates. Deadlines. Such depressing words to describe an exciting process. Many items on the Master List have built-in deadlines. All of the services, electrical, telecommunications, lead retrieval, for instance have them, as do advertisement opportunities.

Others depend on circumstances. The ship date depends on the targeted move in and how long it takes your truck or van line to get to the convention center. The day you start planning the advertisement depends on when materials are due. It also depends on how quickly your graphic artist and copywriter can produce, and how long the internal approval process takes.

One thing's for sure: the Master List can make or break your trade show. A poorly planned list, one with conflicting or unrealistic deadlines, can kill an event, and severely injure the trade show manager's career.

A well-planned Master List makes the job easier. It allows for unforeseen events. It saves the company money. It lets you manage a multiple show schedule. It helps you stay ahead of the game.

Your Master List

Start by constructing your own Master List. Use the one presented earlier in this chapter as a basis. Every company has a different way of doing things, so feel free to add your own processes. And, no, twelve months before the show is not too early.

A three-column format works well—one for the item, one for the start date and one for the deadline. For more control and post-game analysis, add a few more columns. By noting when you actually complete the task, and making comments, you'll be one step ahead in your post event report.

Start Filling It In

Wherever possible, write in *established deadlines*. You already know the show dates. You probably have self-imposed deadlines for things like selecting the space and signing the agreement. Write these in.

Next, enter *estimated deadlines*. Service requests and payment are usually due two to three weeks before the show. The request and payment for lead retrieval rental, about four weeks prior to opening day. Plug these into your List. Be sure to mark them "estimated". As soon as you receive your exhibitor's manual, go back and enter the correct deadlines.

Here's the fun part. *Plan backwards*. That's right. Start at the end of the List, and work your way back, setting deadlines as you go. For instance, you know the show opens on Tuesday, October 3rd. Targeted move in is probably no later than Friday, September 29th. The show is in New York and your company is in Southern California. Your van line tells you they can make the trip in seven days. Fridays are a zoo in your shipping department, so you plan to ship on Thursday, September 21st. And so on. Start with the end in mind.

Sample Master List

To Do	Start	End	Completed	Comments
Select space				
Sign space rental agreement				
Guest Pass order form				
Exhibit description/product locator				
Exhibit description/web site listing				
Exhibit description in Show Preview/Daily				
Exhibitor badge				
Exhibit guide ad insertion order				
Exhibit guide logo form				
Show guide ad materials due				
Exhibit guide logo due				
Begin exhibit guide ad				
Complete exhibit guide ad				
Begin planning pre-show PR				
Plan press kit				
Write news release/backgrounder				
Slides for press kit				
Prepare press kit				
"Best of Show Award" application				
Major signage				
Travel arrangements				
Hotel reservations				
Ground transportation				
Plan/produce new exhibit				
Refurbish exhibit				
Plan display products				
Produce display products				
Update/print collateral materials				
Lead retrieval system, order				
Electrical service, order				
Telecommunications service, order				
Carpet and padding, order				
Furniture, order				
Booth cleaning, order				
I&D Labor, order				
Exhibitor Appointed Contractor (EAC) form				
Freight handling form				
Shipping information form				
Payment/credit card auth/order recap form				
Plan booth staff schedule				
Lights out request form				
Schedule the shipment				
Prepare loose materials				
Prepare exhibit to ship				
Prepare display products				
Prepare shipment				
Ship				
Targeted move-in				
Set-up				
Show dates/hours				
Dismantle				
Receive return materials				

The trade show Master List must coordinate with the rest of the marketing schedule. You need to make sure there are no schedule conflicts. Especially when you are coordinating several shows in a given year.

Sample Budget Worksheet

Item	Estimated	Actual Cost	Comments
Space rental			
Advertising			
Ad space			
Design/Materials			
Copy			
Subtotal			
PR			
Copy writing			
Slide reproduction			
Agency fees			
Other			
Subtotal			
Direct Mail			
Design			
Materials			
Copy			
Printing			
Mailing list			
Postage			
Other			
Subtotal			
Collateral materials			
Design/materials			
Copy writing			
Printing			
Subtotal			
Travel and hotel			
Airfare			
Hotel			
Ground transportation			
Other			
Subtotal			
Shipping (round trip)			
Subtotal			
Show services			
Freight handling			
Labor-set-up & tear-down			
Lead retrieval			
Electrical			
Telecommunications			
Carpet			
Furniture			
Cleaning			
Other			
Subtotal			

Item	Estimated	Actual Cost	Comments
Exhibit			
Rental			
Fabrication			
Repair/refurbishment			
Graphics/Signage			
Other			
Subtotal			
Total expenses			

Visual Props-Using a Yearly or Quarterly Planner

Trade shows have an irritating habit of clustering around certain times of the year. Lots of shows take place in March or April. Others are scheduled around October and November. The problem is—exhibitors run into time crunches when they start exhibiting at several shows a year. It's not uncommon for a company to have a week or less between shows. This is where planning gets tricky.

It's time to invest in a yearly planner, the kind that hangs on the wall. Quarterly planners work, but you'll need all four, and they take up a lot of space. Whichever kind you get, make sure that it has every imaginable holiday clearly marked.

Armed with a Master List for each show, write in all of the show dates for the year. As you do so, you draw a picture of your trade show schedule. It is a graphic that illustrates possible problem areas in your schedule. Add in major deadlines for logistics and you have a clearer picture of just when to schedule things such as exhibit refurbishment. If there is room, include major advertising and PR deadlines. The result is a visual prop to be used as a constant reminder of the big picture.

Using the Exhibitor's Manual

Most large trade shows send out the exhibitor's manual two and a half months before the show. One or two large shows start sending out kits and exhibitor materials as early as four months ahead. If you are exhibiting at regional or tabletop shows, start checking your mailbox at two months.

Trade show management usually mails the kit to the person who signed the space rental agreement. So, if that's not you, make sure the kit is forwarded to you. Call your account executive and ask her to direct the kit to you.

Information on marketing opportunities such as show guide advertisements, sponsorships, on-line pressrooms and virtual exhibits, are sent separately. Some shows mail out a basic folder containing information. Others put together elaborate marketing kits. All trade shows follow up with sales calls.

With the advancement and accessibility of the Internet, most large shows allow you to place your orders, submit your show guide listings and plan your marketing strategies on-line.

Whichever method you use—mail, fax or the Internet—make sure you keep paper copies of every contract and form you submit. You'll need them during set-up and dismantle. Also, they are a handy planning reference the next time you exhibit at that show.

Tracking the Budget with Master List

Planning the trade show budget is like planning a vacation. You can make the travel arrangements and book the hotel, but you can't control the weather. You always end up spending more than you planned.

Many of the expenses involved in exhibiting at a trade show are fixed. That is, they are what they are, and they don't change. Things like exhibit space rental, electrical service, booth cleaning and furniture rental won't change. Once you know your requirements, and how much each service costs, you know what your total expenditures are. The trick is to know how much a service costs before it is available for order.

It is prudent to plot a budget at least 12 months before the trade show. Yet the only figure etched in stone is the cost of the exhibit space. To estimate the cost of show services, you need the exhibitor and marketer's kits. To estimate the cost of travel and lodging, you need to know how much airline and hotel reservations will cost six or eight months from now.

Ideally, your company exhibited at the trade show, or a similar one, in the last year or two. You or your predecessor left a wonderfully complete file, full of contracts, forms, pictures of the exhibit, *and*—a spreadsheet of the budget. Presto! You have a template for this year's budget.

Some rates, such as those for electrical, telecommunications, cleaning and labor, change little from year to year. So it's easy to draw up an estimated budget, as much as a year before the show. You can even estimate the cost of the company's marketing effort, things like advertisement design, collateral materials and direct mail.

But if this is your first show, or the company doesn't keep financial records for marketing expenses, then you will have to start from scratch. You *can* generate estimates for almost every item on the Master List. It may take some time, some phone calls, even a well placed gift. But it can be done.

Trade Show Services, Shipping and Marketing Opportunities

These are the easiest items for which to obtain costs. If your company exhibited at the show within the past few years, you may be able to dig up some figures. Even if a spreadsheet was never generated, the accounting department keeps records of every payment. So roll up your sleeves, schmooze the accounts payable manager and get to work. Arm yourself with information about the previous trade show: dates, location, exhibition service and marketing opportunities such as advertisements and sponsorships.

While you are digging through accounts payable records, look for trucking company invoices going to and from the show site. Track down invoices for travel and hotel, too. These figures are the most likely to change from year to year. But it's nice to have an idea of the cost, even if it's a rough one.

If this is your first trade show, there are other resources available. Call the account representative of a particular trade show. They might have exhibitor and marketer's kits from last year's show, and it won't hurt to ask. What the representative *will* have, are the names and numbers of vendors who *can* give you the financial information. Each service and marketing vendor can tell you last year's going rate. They may even have a collection of last year's order forms. Make sure you have handy your company's booth number, because they won't share information with just anyone. They will want to know you are exhibiting at the next show.

Once you know the unit price of last year's services at the show you're on your way to generating a pretty good estimate of this year's budget.

Costs for freight handling, labor and shipping vary widely from year to year. Not because vendors raise the rates, but because other variables pop up. Maybe your exhibit is bigger, heavier, and more expensive to ship, handle and set up. Maybe your trucker has to wait in line at the loading dock one year, passing the expense on to you. Maybe set-up falls on a holiday this year, and you end up paying double time for labor.

Collateral Materials, Direct Mail, Advertising and News Releases

The printer, graphic artist and copywriter—all work to produce materials for the show. And they all get paid. Some of these services may be performed in-house and can't be directly accounted for in your budget. But things like printing and certain aspects of ad design should go on your estimate.

Your printer can give you an estimate for the cost to reproduce brochures and data sheets. If you set aside only half of the print run for the show, charge only half the cost to your estimated budget. If the materials need to be updated, be sure to figure in the cost to produce new film. Most printers still use film to produce the final product.

The show guide advertisement also requires a set of film and a matchprint. The matchprint is simply a top-quality glossy printout of the ad, using the film. Printers use it to exactly match the colors and to tell them what the ad or brochure should look like.

It is much harder to estimate the design costs, if you've never used an outside graphic artist, agency or design firm. All are loath to give out blind estimates for advertisements and brochures. They prefer to give full proposals. When you request those estimates, be sure to account for the cost of photography.

A well-written news release makes all the difference. Fees for ad concepts and writing are relatively easy to estimate. Count on anywhere from $200 to $600 for a news release, whether you use an agency or freelancer. Ask the freelancer, agency or design firm for their fee schedule.

Exhibit Property

If you rent your exhibit, the cost estimate is as close as the phone. There are plenty of resources for renting. The products are all quite similar and so are the costs. The same is true if you are buying a new or used prefabricated exhibit. Costs increase as you add graphics.

Building a custom exhibit is a different story. Costs vary widely, depending on the design, materials and labor involved. The sensible thing to do is to have a budget in mind when you hire the fabricator. If this is your first exposure to building your own, you may find yourself adjusting your expectations, or your budget—so think in terms of plus or minus five or ten thousand dollars.

If you already own your exhibit, you still need to account for occasional repair and refurbishment. Even under ideal conditions, your exhibit will need plastic surgery every couple of years.

Cheat Sheet

Planning is the key to managing a great trade show. However, all the planning in the world won't save you from disaster if you don't stick your schedule. Because trade show tasks are spread out over a 12-month period, it is vital to plot a detailed course of action well in advance.

Plotting is crucial when your company exhibits in several shows during a calendar year. There are a number of tools and tricks for getting and staying organized.

Here's what you learned in this chapter:

•Using a master "to do" list.

- How to set deadlines.
- Using a yearly or quarterly planner as a visual aid.
- How to use the exhibitor's manual.
- How to estimate your budget.

4
How to Have a Great Exhibit

It's Sunday night, the kids are in bed, and your mate has nodded off. So now you're in control of the television and more importantly—the remote. Life is good. You change channels until you find your favorite movie.

Opening credits, music, a great opening scene. And then a boring advertisement! Instinctively, you start to surf the channels. A woman doing laundry. Click. A woman yelling at the camera. It's that confusing public service ad. Click. Some guy dressed up as a bumble-bee, yelling. Click.

A man dressed as a doctor. Interesting accent, just like the one in the movie that won all the awards last year. He's talking defensively into the telephone. What's he saying? Is this a dentist's office? Sounds like he's talking to a police officer. The man in the waiting room looks worried. Probably about the dentist. Oh, this is so funny! It's an advertisement about a hotel chain. Click. Back to the movie.

Lots of people ignore the ads on television. Their minds are saturated with the thousands of messages. But, sometimes they watch. Something about the ad makes the viewer pay attention.

Trade show exhibits are great big ads. They are three-dimensional ads that make attendees (viewers) stop and pay attention. Something about the exhibit makes them want to walk through it, read signs, look at products and touch the displays. So piqued is their interest, they want to know more. Ideally, they end up purchasing the exhibitor's product.

Looks Count

Television advertisements only have five seconds to capture the viewer's interest. After that, the viewer is on to something else. They surf channels, fix a snack or go to the bathroom. Clicking through hundreds of images and experiences competing with each other for the viewer's attention—and money.

A good ad, like the one that reeled in our Sunday night viewer, doesn't waste time. It opens with an interesting hook, something slightly familiar yet with the promise of a payoff. It tells a story with memorable characters and setting. It has an identifiable message and an easy-to-follow theme. The ad leaves the viewer with a feeling (amused), an opinion about the company (hip), and the belief that using the product will benefit her in a specific way.

The task of trade show exhibits is similar to that of television advertisements. Sure, attendees may be more motivated to purchase or recommend than television viewers. Attendees pay good money and go to considerable trouble to show up. Trade shows help them keep up to date on the latest products and services. But you still compete for their attention.

Your exhibit is one of hundreds. You are up against all sorts of live action presentations, video walls, professional performers, elaborate give-aways, catered brunches, and endless attention-getting gimmicks. This is not to say you must put on an elaborate show. But you *do* have to wrestle for attendee mind-share.

Once you have their attention, you need to make a lasting impression. A specific impression. One that tells them who the company is and what they do. Most importantly, one that leaves the attendee with the impression: "I like this company. I like their product. I *need* their product."

This is as important for your existing customers as it is for people who are unfamiliar with your company. Trade shows are one of the few opportunities established customers have to get up close and personal with the company and its representatives. It is an opportunity to size your company up, so to speak. It is *your* opportunity to cement the relationship. Attendees who visit your exhibit end up with a specific impression of your company. Make it a favorable one.

Checklist for a Great Exhibit

Joe Client is a long-time customer. The Small Fry, Inc. salesman developed Joe's account through cold calls and visits. Joe knows the company through occasional advertisements and his own experience. He's formed an opinion of the company. They sell decent products, they are easy to deal with, although their new ordering system is more complicated. Joe could get the product from Major Distributor, Inc., at a lower cost, but would the after-sales support be as good?

Joe makes a point to stop by Small Fry Inc.'s exhibit. It is a professional looking booth, easy to locate, colorful, and contemporary. By the time he leaves the exhibit, he has a strong impression of the company's focus and capabilities. Small Fry, Inc. is innovative, an industry leader, customer-oriented, stable. Joe feels confident about keeping his business right where it is.

Attendees who've never done business with Small Fry, Inc., flow in and out of the exhibit. They leave with the same positive impression. Even people who never heard of the company manage to find the exhibit and come away with the same bright image.

What did the Small Fry, Inc. trade show manager do to create such a great and memorable impact? He knew his company's mission statement, corporate identity and market. He created an attention-getting exhibit that communicated the message. When he sat down to plan the exhibit, he asked himself a few questions:

Does the overall design tell attendees who the company is and what they do? The company's name and logo should be visible and obvious to anyone passing by the exhibit. The casual passer-by should also be able to tell what products or services the company offers. The best test? If you could grab a stranger off the street, a volunteer, blindfold him and stand him in front of the fully decorated exhibit—give him five seconds to look before whisking him away, how much would he be able to tell about the company? Would he remember its name? What they sell?

Does the design send a specific message to the attendees? Not just any message. The right message. Most companies have mottoes, or taglines. These taglines boil the mission statement down into a few memorable words. For example, the company who makes hardware that connects computers over networks and the Internet might have a tagline like, "We connect you to the world." Companies often have a secondary message, a quality such as reliability, stability, innovation, technology leader, high tech and so on. So, do the exhibit's colors say "high tech"? What about the shapes and forms used in the exhibit walls? Would that volunteer have a clear sense of the company's message?

Is it esthetically pleasing? Designing an exhibit is like planning a wedding: all of the colors and materials must coordinate with one another. And although we may never understand the psychology behind poofy-sleeved antebellum bride's maid dresses, we must consider psychology when choosing colors and shades for the exhibit.

Does it showcase the company's products and or services? It is one thing to plunk down your products on a table, and quite another to use the display to capture interest. Product displays need to be as interactive as possible. Even a display for services needs to draw the attendee in, so that he participates in some way. If possible, have your products performing their tasks. You might also consider, at regular intervals, demonstrating the product's wondrous abilities.

Having your product open and available to attendees to look at and touch is an excellent way to hook purists and technophyles—and specifiers.

Presentations also add an experiential element to service-oriented products, and context to physical products.

When showing products, don't pile them all on one table. Putting distance between them helps attendees keep them straight so that they remember them later. Consider that the more products you cram into your exhibit, the less memorable individual ones become.

Is it attendee-friendly? A successful exhibit is laid out in a way that allows foot traffic to flow easily into the space. It is open enough to let attendees move about without feeling claustrophobic. Placing displays around the exhibit's perimeter creates a barrier that tends to keep attendees out, rather than corralling them in. So, use interesting displays, signs and demonstrations to keep attendees in your exhibit. Keep enough space between them to allow staff and attendees room in which to gather.

Is it staff-friendly? A successful exhibit is one that sets up with a minimum of fuss. It a sensible set-up-friendly design and the plans are accessible and easy to follow. The exhibit creates a comfortable work environment for staffers without turning them into couch potatoes. Carpet padding is an absolute necessity for staffers *and* attendees who spend many hours on their feet. There should be enough counter space for things like lead retrieval, paper work, business cards and collateral materials. You need adequate storage for materials such as office supplies, brochures, and personal items like purses and backpacks.

Do signs attract attendees at several distances? An exhibit isn't an exhibit without signs. Signs are designed to capture attention from three different groups of attendees: those who are far away — several aisles over; those who are nearby — somewhere on the same aisle; and those who are inside of the exhibit.

Bird's-eye-view signs perched atop the exhibit announce the company's presence to folks on the exhibit floor. These are known as *headers*. The taller the exhibit and header, the farther afield the announcement can be seen. Signs hanging from the ceiling above the exhibit are visible throughout the exhibit hall. Headers and hanging signs are simply the company's name, logo, and possibly its tagline.

Attendees walking in the aisle can easily see and read poster-sized signs. At least part of the sign may be above eye level. It contains a longer message and graphics. The text is large enough for someone standing in the aisle to read. It is short and to the point.

Eye level signs are aimed at folks browsing the exhibit, perhaps looking at a display. The text is smaller, though usually at least 14 point. The message is more detailed and its goal more specific. These are the signs used to identify the display product.

One, two, three. Signs placed higher on the booth have simper, more obvious messages aimed at attracting attendees from far away. Signs placed above eye level have a more elaborate message aimed at attracting attendees into the booth. Signs at eye level are more detailed and attract attendees in the booth to particular displays.

To Rent or to Own: The Big Question

One of the first questions you need to answer is whether you are going to rent the exhibit property or to own an exhibit. To answer this question, ask yourself a few more.

How often are you going to use it? If you only exhibit at a few shows per year, renting is an economical choice. Each time you rent an exhibit, you pay somewhere in the neighborhood of one quarter to one third the cost of actually designing and building the same property. This does not include the cost of storing the exhibit between trade shows. Nor does it account for repairs or refurbishing.

If you exhibit at less than three trade shows in a given year, renting is a good way to go. If you exhibit at more than three, owning is an attractive option. If you exhibit at 12 or more shows, consider that you may need to either own your exhibit *and* rent a second one, or own two complete exhibits.

Can you afford to store the exhibit between trade shows? If you have the space and the personnel to handle the property you may choose to store the exhibit at your own facility.

Another option is to rent storage space off site. Again, a good option if you have the personnel and equipment to handle the property, but lack the space to store it.

A third option is to store the property with the exhibit builder. Established companies offer storage and handling services for a fee. It is more expensive than storing the exhibit yourself. But these folks specialize in storing and handling exhibit properties. They will end up doing it more efficiently. They will also inventory and inspect your exhibit for damage after each event—for a fee.

Are you willing and able to keep your exhibit in good repair? Depending on the type of exhibit, how often you use it, and how gently it is handled during shipping and drayage, exhibits need periodic repair and refurbishment.

Treated well, most exhibits go at least a year before they need a facelift. Usually around year two or three, a well designed and cared-for property starts to show its age.

Whichever you choose, to rent or to own, you are responsible for creating and maintaining your own graphics. And you will change these more often than you refurbish or redesign your exhibit.

In short, the more often you exhibit, the better off you are owning your own exhibit. The larger and more complicated your exhibit, the better off you are storing it with your fabricator. The more you rely on trade shows to support your corporate image, the more valuable are great graphics and exhibits.

Exhibit Crafting 101

Whether you rent or own, there are many types of exhibits from which to choose. An exhibit may be as simple as a few tables and chairs, or as elaborate as a multiple story solid structure.

Bargain basement. The least expensive exhibit is none at all. For a few hundred dollars, you can rent tables, a few chairs and carpet. Show management offers furniture rental through their officially appointed decorator. The exhibitor's manual contains order forms and descriptions; even photographs of deluxe furniture options.

Since you rent the furniture through the official decorator, you don't spend money to ship an exhibit. Consider this if you are on a tight budget and are renting a 100-square-foot space. This is also a great option if the trade show is a smaller, regional style event. These are typically held in smaller city and hotel convention centers.

Modular panel system. For a few hundred dollars more, you can rent respectable-looking equipment through show management's appointed decorator. With panels, you can build a backwall eight feet tall, and eight-, 10- or 20-feet long. The official decorator offers a limited variety of looks and designs. As an added benefit, you do not have to pay freight. But remember, BYOG— bring your own graphics, and make sure they are compatible with the system's construction.

With an outside source, you *do* pay freight, but you have more models and better quality to choose from. This is a great option for 100-, 200-, and 400-square-foot **in-line** exhibits.

Portable "pop-ups". The world is teeming with companies who offer stock exhibits for rent or purchase. These off-the-shelf properties are ready-made and need very little change to suit individual exhibitors. Lightweight portables are set up and dismantled by one or two staffers in less than half an hour.

Popular models supply a sleek, curved backwall. They work like this: You and your buddy cruise into your booth space. You pop the lid off the exhibit's shipping container. Next, you pull out the ultra-light metallic frame and pop it up—expanding it to full size. Attach the exterior and graphics and voila, you have a beautiful eight-foot tall, ten-foot wide backwall (it's a little more complicated than this, but not much.)

You save money because you don't need labor. In fact, you save money on shipping, because it is much lighter than standard prefabricated exhibits.

Backwalls are available in eight-foot, ten-foot and 20-foot widths. You can add matching countertops and display stands. The coolest option is the **self-contained exhibit**, in which the shipping container converts to a countertop.

Portable pop-ups range from full back walls to small table-top displays. The smaller version is identical to its big brother, but at one or two feet in height, it fits neatly on a table.

Pop-ups overlap modular panel systems in rental costs. A nice backwall with one or two display stands starts at under a thousand dollars. By the time you've rented the system three or four times, you've spent enough to buy it. Of course, you don't have to pay to store it between shows. And you don't have to spend time and money to repair it.

Whether you rent or own, pop-ups are perfect for 100- and 200-square-foot **in-line** exhibit spaces.

Prefabricated stock. Now we're getting into the big leagues. Prefab stock takes up where modular panel systems leave off. Here you buy or rent an exhibit that is basically "off-the-shelf". You go into the showroom, look at the floor models, or flip through the catalogue and say, "I'll take that one."

All set up, your own graphics in place, the exhibit gives a professional impression. Prefab stock range from a modest centerpiece and matching product display counters to an elaborate center tower with connecting display stands and work counters. The skyline can be eight feet, all the way to up to 20 feet. In fact, you can increase your floor space with a multiple story "double-decker".

The exhibit can be constructed from lightweight aluminum framing and fabric, or laminated wood. You can choose from a number of wonderful designs to exhibit in 100-, 400-, 10,000-square-foot spaces and more. Prefab stock exhibits are perfect for companies who want a grand exhibit without having to purchase. For the company who prefers to own, new or used, they are a great alternative.

Custom exhibits. These are the top of the line for companies who want to buy an exhibit designed just for them. The exhibit projects the company's personality. It advances a specific marketing agenda. It *looks* like a custom exhibit.

The range is broad. You can spend five thousand or five hundred thousand dollars or more. You can have a conventional-looking exhibit, or you can buy something innovative.

Do you want to promote your athletic foot apparel company? How about an exhibit that looks like a giant tennis shoe? Want to tell the world you're a major player ready to serve? Try a theme-based 1950's-style boxcar diner. Want a simple, sleek look that says "cutting-edge" and "trustworthy"? That's okay too.

You can have a small, *custom modular panel* or *custom portable* system designed to set up in a variety of configurations—100-, 200- or 400-square feet.

The possibilities are endless. The best news is, if you are careful choosing the design and materials, you can have a custom exhibit for just a little more than a stock prefab. The key is in finding the right exhibit fabricator. More on that later in chapter 3.

Owning: Comparing Costs

Under $3,000—Portable pop-up displays
Under $10,000—Modular panel systems
$8,000 and above—Stock and custom exhibits

Putting it All Together: Three Configurations

Backwall with display stands. If your exhibit space is an in-line (faces one aisle), corner (faces two aisles), or peninsular or end-cap (faces three aisles), you'll be using a backwall configuration. As long as you share at least one wall with another exhibitor, you need a backwall.

All 80- and 100-square foot booths are in-line or corner exhibits. Most 200-square-foot booths are simply two in-lines combined. Peninsular booths, which share only one wall with another exhibitor, are usually 400-square feet. Occasionally, you will see a 600-square-foot peninsular booth. These exhibits are typically no taller than eight feet. They are portable pop-ups or modular panel systems, either stock or custom designs.

Configuring a small exhibit is tricky. The backwall takes up a chunk of space, but you need a reception counter where you can talk to prospects and take leads. At best, you can comfortably exhibit two products in the 100-square-foot space, and four or five in a 200-square-foot exhibit.

Central tower with display counters. It's very liberating—an island booth open to aisles on all four sides. No walls to share. More freedom for creative designs, more space for displays. Instead of a backwall, the tower structure becomes the central focus. A tower is a construction that rises up 12 to 20 feet, usually at the center of the exhibit. The design possibilities are endless, from a simple cylinder to an Eiffel Tower look-alike. With your corporate logo on its top and graphics on the walls, the tower serves triple duty.

One important duty is as a beacon to prospects far and near. The taller the tower, the more visible its logo from the farthest aisles. A tower also functions as a visual anchor for the entire exhibit. A third function is as a place to hang some graphics. Two more perks—the tower's base is a great place to add a few counters for displays or workspace. And its interior makes a great storage area.

To extend their message, many exhibitors add smaller towers where more graphics drive home the point. Graphics towers also help balance the exhibit visually.

Some well-placed display counters and a reception counter round out the exhibit. One excellent configuration combines a graphics tower with the display counter.

And there you have the plot for a basic tower configuration. Add an enclosed conference area and you have somewhere to sit with a few special prospects, somewhere to make a personalized sales pitch, crunch a few numbers and close a sale or two.

Islands with tower-style exhibits run as small as 400-square-feet and as large as the largest booth spaces—more than 36,000-square-feet.

Themed and specialty exhibits. These are the faux shops for the makers of fine china and crystal. The exhibit made to look like a mini football stadium for the athletic apparel company. The 50's-style diner for the digital messaging company. The list goes on and on.

The majority are custom designs and, like the tower style, work well in medium to large booth spaces. You can spend a lot of money on such exhibits, but you can also put together good-looking themed exhibits on a tight budget. It all depends on the theme, and on the image you want to create. What's more, you can add themed elements to an existing exhibit, creating a hybrid.

For example, a few years ago Sun Microsystems introduced its new web authoring language using trade shows as its launch vehicle. The company added a coffee service to its exhibit, complete with a beautiful brass dispenser, trained attendants and a selection to rival the finest gourmet shop. The company's new product was Java, now an essential web authoring tool.

Other ways exhibitors add themes to their exhibits: provide a catered wine and cheese service, a clown act, a magic act, or a dog and pony show. Well, maybe not the dog and pony thing, but you get the picture.

Themes can use a gimmick that is guaranteed to pull prospects into your exhibit. However, not all prospects are "qualified". The better the gimmick, the more time you spend weeding out the wine drinkers and magician fans.

Themes can also be a creative variation on the company's marketing campaign. The inside of a high-end shop for a china and crystal company, java service for Java service. Still a lot of pizzazz, but a more targeted message. You may not necessarily pull throngs through the exhibit, but you *will* increase foot traffic. And off they go, back to their offices, with a memorable experience that matches your message.

Two things to remember as you plan your special exhibit. One, keep a close eye on the budget. It's easy for everyone involved in planning to get so excited about the theme that they over-spend. And two, keep the other eye on convention center regulations. It'll break more than your heart if you've built an exhibit that breaks their rules.

Owning Your Own Exhibit

So, you're company decided to buy an exhibit. You have a number of options, depending on your budget. Buying used property keeps the purchase price down. But be ready to spend money to make repairs. You may also want to modify the exhibit—make it more "you". And, new or used, custom or a ready-made, you still need to add graphics.

You've had the meetings, formed the committees and now you are ready to do it. You are ready to price portable pop-ups. Or you want find a good used modular panel system. Perhaps you are ready for a new custom exhibit. Do you pull out your yellow pages?

For Sale: Where to Find Them

The *phone book* is a great place to start, if you are located in a major metropolitan area. Look under "Trade Shows, Expositions & Fairs."

The best place to find companies who rent and sell exhibits is the *Internet*. Naturally. There are two ways to find them: through the search engine's Yellow Pages, or by a global search using a keyword or phrase.

The beauty of using the *on-line Yellow Pages* is that you can create a list of exhibit companies near you. Some of the companies that cranked out during the search won't have offices near you, but they want to do business with you just the same. Some are headquartered elsewhere, with local offices near you. And most of them will be resellers rather than original manufacturers.

To build a list, call up your favorite search engine's Yellow Pages and plug in "Display Designers and Producers." As a bonus, the search may crank out names of other accomplices, such as lighting experts and hanging sign manufacturers.

A *keyword global search* on your favorite search engine spits out pages of entries. Again, you have to sort them out, to find a fabricator that fits your needs. On the up side, with the click of the mouse, you can go from the entry to the fabricator's web site. On the down side, some fabricators aren't on the Internet yet. The perfect one might be just across town. But you won't find it if you only rely on a keyword search.

Another great way to find contenders for the job is through trade show industry publications and their web sites. Two of the most helpful magazines, as of this writing, are *Exhibitor*, and its web site, *exhibitornet.com*; and *Tradeshow Week*, and *tradeshowweek.com*. Both publications provide lists of trade show related service providers on their web sites. Fabricators also advertise in print editions.

But when all is said and done, the ideal way to find a fabricator is through *personal referral*. Your advertising or PR agencies are likely sources. If you've seen a trade show exhibit you particularly like, call its owner and ask who built it.

Choosing a Fabricator

So, who are you going to hire to design and build your exhibit? Who will you trust with 10-, 30-, 50-thousand dollars or more of your company's money? Every company has its own criteria for selecting service providers. Here are a few more questions to consider.

Where are the actual fabrication facilities? The ideal situation is for the facilities to be within an hour to an hour and a half drive from your office. That way you can do a site inspection before hiring them. You can pop in to see how everything is going. View the product. Regrettably, this isn't always possible.

If the facility is not accessible, you must rely on the fabricator's progress reports and photographs.

What are their resources? How much floor space is in the construction area? How many work areas, how many exhibits can they work on at one time? How many designers on staff? What sort of drafting equipment do they use? Essentially, you are interested in how well equipped they are to design and build your exhibit. Limited facilities, limited abilities.

What is their experience? How long have these folks been designing and building trade show exhibits? Trade show exhibits are highly specialized items. A company has to be up-to-date on not only design trends, but also materials, lighting techniques, convention hall rules and regulations, and shipping container design and deployment. These folks aren't just service providers or craftsmen. They are your partners in a high profile venture.

What other services do they offer? Some fabricators do more than just design and build exhibits. Many also keep inventory, inspect, ship, receive, and warehouse properties, as well as assist clients in coordinating and ordering services. For a fee, of course. And for the busy exhibitor, these services are worth every penny.

What have they done lately? Take a good look at their portfolio. Most fabricators offer a sample portfolio on their web site. You need to be sure they can do what they claim.

What do their customers have to say about them? Call up some of the company's clients and ask them about their experiences with the fabricator. And don't leave off with the official client list. Ask around your industry. Call your ad agency, your friends in your professional association, your former colleagues over at XYZ Corp. Ask if they've heard anything, good or bad, about the fabricator. Call the Better Business Bureau in their city, ask if any complaints have been filed against them, and if so, how were they resolved.

Will they last? Some companies ask to see the fabricator's financial statement. When they are investing a lot of time and money in a project, the company wants to know that the fabricator won't fold before completing the project.

Pump Up the Volume: Presentations

Your exhibit is fabulous, your graphics are fabulous, and your product displays are fabulous. Everything is fabulous. Can it get any better than this? What if you could double, even triple your foot traffic? What if you could add an element to your exhibit that would buy, in one hour, as many qualified leads as your booth personnel squeeze out in one day? Would you do it?

What if that new element doubled your exhibit costs? Would you do it then? Tough question. Presentations can cost a few hundred, a few thousand or a few hundred thousand dollars. But if it helps land a large contract or two, it might be worth it.

Trade show presentations are an art form and the methods available to trade show managers today are varied. They can be as simple as one of your salesmen giving a scripted product demonstration or as complex as a theatrical production. Every year, advancing technology add new capabilities to their services. Here is an introduction to this complex, ever changing subject.

Entertainment

You can hire a magician or a clown to perform in your exhibit. Theoretically, the juggling or card tricks or balloon animals lure people to your exhibit and into your hands. Your booth personnel turn them into leads. Unfortunately, the increased foot traffic doesn't translate into lots of hot prospects. You simply get more leads to sift through at the end of the show.

Live Presentations and Demonstrations

A small stage, ten chairs, audiovisual equipment and a slide show. Add your best salesperson and a five-minute speech, and you have a basic presentation with great potential. There are many variations on this theme. Product demonstrations instead of the slide show. A big stage and a larger audience.

For this basic set up, you rent the equipment—stage, chairs, and audiovisual equipment. Write the short script and design the slide show, or outsource the creative work. You have the option of hiring professional talent to make the presentation.

Keep the presentation between five and seven minutes in length. More than seven and you risk boring your audience. Less than five and you won't leave them with a memorable impression. Also, make sure people know when to show up for the presentation. A nice clock sign with a message, "Next show at 10 am" is fine. If you can mention the presentation in your advertising, do it.

Multimedia Presentations

Another classic form of presentation is multimedia. You don't need to tie up one of your salespeople or hire a presenter. You're not even limited to five-minute presentations once an hour, or once every two hours. Multimedia presentations can be a continuous experience for attendees that leave your exhibit staff free to concentrate on qualifying prospects.

A basic multimedia presentation uses a kiosk—a monitor or video screen with sound, and cabinet—and content. The content can be a simple slide show, video and graphical presentation with 3D animation. A touch screen LCD lets you present an interactive program.

You are renting more equipment, creating fancier graphics and spending more money than you do for a simple live presentation. But you get to be more creative. What's more, the multimedia presentation fits neatly on a CD to make a great mailer or handout.

Be warned though. There are many, many companies promoting themselves as specialists in multimedia presentations for trade shows. It is one thing to be an expert in programming multimedia software, or to be a great animator or sound integrator. But it is quite another to craft a presentation event that sells your company and product.

Not all multimedia specialists are marketing experts. You'll need an experienced marketer on the team.

Main Stage Productions

This is a top of the line technique and it plays just the way it sounds: A production that takes place on a main stage. The presentation turns into an event, a performance. An event-marketing expert creates a concept and works with a writer, creative director and producer to stage a presentation guaranteed to awe attendees.

A main stage production can be a straight presentation performed with lights and sound effects or it can be a "Who Wants To Be A Millionaire" look-alike. Just make sure the production focuses on selling the company and its product.

This is an expensive venture. It's not much different from producing a television advertisement, complete with actors. If you plan to add a staged production to your exhibit, take the time to educate yourself. Observe a few for yourself. Talk to exhibitors who've gone the main stage route. Get references.

A Few Words about Shipping Containers

After the excitement of designing the exhibit, choosing colors and looking at laminate, who wants to think about shipping containers? Crates, cartons, boxes—boring, right? Not to a pro.

Anyone who has managed a few shows finds the subject quite fascinating. Picture this: You arrive at the convention center ready to set up your exhibit. You pick your way through the litter of unrolled carpets and skyscraper crates. You find your booth and inspect your property.

The good news is—it's all there. Everything arrived. The bad news is—there's a big hole in one of your shipping containers. Down near the bottom, about the size of a forklift prong. Yes, your exhibit has been forked. You complain to the people in charge of moving exhibits and equipment within the convention center, and they complain to you about the container's design. They are not liable for the damage, they say, according to the contract you signed, and lifelong fascination with shipping containers is born.

Your exhibit's survival depends on this drab construction. It depends on having the appropriate container, the right design and the highest quality of construction. There are several issues to consider when choosing your shipping containers.

Size. If the container or containers are too large, you will have a tough time transporting them by airfreight. Large containers fit in only the largest jets. Jumbo jets depart from and land at only the largest airports. If you absolutely, positively have to get your exhibit across the country three days hence, you'll have better luck if your containers are small enough to fit on smaller aircraft.

If the containers are too small, you'll have a tough time packing and tracking them. To a certain degree, the size and shape of your exhibit's components dictate the size and shape of the containers. The smaller they are, the tighter the fit. The more containers you have, the easier it is for your shipper to lose them

Dimensions. The right shape makes all the difference when it comes to shipping the exhibit. Containers need to be crafted in such a way that they fit easily into a wide variety of transport vehicles.

Airlines take your exhibit containers and pack them into larger bins, which are tailored to their aircraft. If your containers are an odd dimension, very tall or wide, they won't meet the airline's criteria.

The same holds true for ground transport. If it is at all possible, have your shipping containers designed so that they fit neatly into the cargo area of a small truck. Your van line uses an 18-wheeler to haul your exhibit 1,000 miles. But they may send a smaller vehicle to pick it up from your warehouse.

Popular Shipping Containers			
Type	Benefits	Drawbacks	When to Use
Wooden crate	Offers the best protection for your exhibit.	Its weight adds significantly to shipping costs (as much as 1/3.)	Use with heavy exhibits that have wooden panels.
Plastic tubs	Light weight, durable and easy to handle. Keeps shipping costs down	Costlier than wood crate (to purchase.)	Light weight portable exhibits.
Reusable containers/ A.T.A.-style flight cases	Much lighter than wood, wheels make it easier to move around.	Costlier than wood crate (to purchase.) Less durable than tubs. wood, or plastic	Lightweight portable exhibits, small panel systems. Not suitable for large, heavy exhibits.

Portability. If the container is too heavy for one guy to handle, it's going to spend some time on a forklift. Exhibit containers need to be designed with feet that provide enough room between the container and the floor for a large forklift's tines.

Some containers are built with rollers that allow them to be wheeled on a smooth cement surface. But these roll-abouts still need a forklift to move them over a long distance, so be sure they have enough ground clearance.

Weight and durability. There are three types of containers and the one you choose is based largely on the specifications of your exhibit. Containers are almost always designed for the exhibit they are to carry.

Wood crates do the best job of protecting your exhibit and they're the least expensive to construct. The down side—they are expensive to ship. Wood crates are heavy, up to one third of the shipment's weight.

Your exhibit crafter can build wood crates. Or you can save money and outsource the job, without sacrificing quality. However, the exhibit crafter is in a better position to tailor a container to your exhibit.

Plastic tubs are the lightest and least expensive to ship. They are not constructed so much as they are "formed", like margarine tubs. Tubs are surprisingly sturdy. About the only thing that breaks or wears out are the straps that lock down their lids.

A.T.A.-style cases, also called flight cases, are a type of reusable container made with sturdy, lightweight material and reinforced with metal. Do you remember High School Band practice? If you or someone you knew played the clarinet, saxophone, tuba or other instrument, then you also remember the carrying cases. A lot of those were A.T.A.-style.

Both A.T.A. cases and plastic tubs are more expensive to purchase than are wood crates. But they can be tailored to a wide range of specifications. They are light, making them less expensive to ship than wood crates. Wheels make it easy to move them short distances, which comes in handy during set-up or when the exhibit is being stored.

A.T.A. cases are great for transporting signage, delicate equipment—especially display products and computers—and set-up supplies. They are also perfect for small, portable exhibits. The larger and heavier the exhibit, though, the less protection they offer.

Picture an exhibit of several long, heavy wooden panels packed without care in a ten-foot-long, four-foot-high A.T.A. case. As big and heavy as it is, the case can be jolted or shoved during transport. Those big heavy panels slide and smack against the case wall and cause damage. And a forklift can gouge a hole in that ten-foot section.

A few last thoughts: pack the exhibit in the case so that nothing slides around. Pack the contents in a tight configuration. Even the most delicate exhibit can survive rough handling if it is correctly packed.

Maintaining the Exhibit

What part of trade show management costs money, takes a lot of time, needs no creativity and in no way shows your boss how valuable you are? If you answered "making sure the exhibit stays in top condition," then you win the prize.

Maintaining the exhibit takes zero creativity, unless you count all the doodling you do while you're on hold—getting repair estimates from the fabricator and the boss's okay to spend the money. But maintenance is an important task.

There is nothing quite like setting up your exhibit at a trade show, and finding a big gash in the backwall, or badly chipped laminate on the countertops. All exhibits, no matter how carefully you handle them, eventually acquire damage. If the exhibit is not well maintained, the company's image suffers.

The best way to handle maintenance is to perform an inventory and inspect each piece of the exhibit after each show. If your exhibit fabricator stores the property for you, have them count the pieces and inspect for damage as soon as they receive it. They will generate a report for your records. Of course, they'll charge you for their effort. That's the "costs money" part. But it's worth it.

If you store the exhibit yourself, you'll need to perform the count and inspection yourself. That's the "takes up a lot of time" part. It's also hard work. And you'll need to list and describe the damage.

It isn't necessary to send the entire exhibit back to its fabricator for repairs. Simply pull out the chipped counter top or damaged panel and ship them solo.

Cheat Sheet

Looks count. There is quite a lot of psychology behind exhibit design and graphics. Size, color and shape all create an image of your company. An exhibit can be attractive and tasteful, yet convey the wrong message.

Exhibits needn't be expensive. Depending on the size and number of trade shows in which you participate, you can rent a wonderful yet cost-effective exhibit. At some point you may want to own some or all of your exhibit property. The key is to choose a great designer and exhibit crafter.

If you own your exhibit property, expect to make minor repairs once a year or so and major repairs every few years. Carpets usually need to be replaced every few years. The most effective way to preserve your exhibit is to use sensible packing and shipping practices. Choose crates that are right for your type of exhibit. Pack carefully every time, even during tear-down.

Here's what we covered in this chapter:

- •Looks count. Exhibits are big three-dimensional advertisements.
- •A great exhibit tells people who you are and what you do. It sends a specific message, is easy to use for attendees and booth staff, and uses signage effectively.
- •Deciding whether to rent or own—the more events in which you exhibit, the more likely you are to own.
- •Owning your exhibit—research the designer and crafter thoroughly.
- •You can increase the effectiveness of your exhibit with presentations and demonstrations.
- •Care in tearing down the exhibit, proper packing and shipping reduces damage and repair costs.

5

All About Graphics and Signs

The interesting thing about putting together a trade show is that the person managing it gains experience in several disciplines. He's in charge of getting the word out to all the important editors whether or not he writes the news releases himself. He makes sure the ads get designed, even if he's colorblind. He must coordinate and manage a cadre of specialists. So he must have arm chair expertise in each area, at the very least.

Hands-on experience isn't necessary, although it certainly helps. Knowing exactly what goes into designing and producing an ad, the process, the materials, even the creativity, lets the manager plan his schedule and budget, and manage the graphic artist with more efficiency. Knowledge is power. It keeps the trade show manager under budget, on time and in control.

PR and advertisements are easy. Or at least, they're not so far afield from the trade show manager's core competency. If you are managing trade shows, you are either a part of your company's marketing department, or you work for a PR or ad agency—providing management services to your clients.

Designing and producing exhibits is a little tougher. But once you find an exhibit builder who does a good job, you're set. The builder helps you design it; he builds it, maybe helps you manage the "property" (that's what we call exhibits in the trade show biz,) cleans it up and repairs it periodically.

But your exhibit's signs and graphics are another matter. The materials and techniques are a little more exotic. Sure, your exhibit producer will help you with them. In fact, graphics are one of the most important elements in your exhibit. But production is a different discipline, therefore exhibit crafters outsource most of the graphics work.

This is a great solution to the graphics problem when you are designing and building a new exhibit. But when it comes time to change graphics and create new signs—and you'll do this many times throughout the exhibit's life—you may want to do it yourself. Cut out the middleman, (the exhibit producer), and go straight to the sign maker or the reprographics company. Or maybe you're putting together a smaller, stock exhibit and you want to produce the graphics and signs yourself.

Whatever the reason, knowing the ins and outs of signs and graphics will give you greater control over the process. It'll impress your friends, colleagues and your boss.

Exhibit Graphics Defined

There are four types of exhibit graphics:

Structural graphics

Your exhibit producer crafts a three-dimensional rendering of your company logo and name—block lettering, to sit atop your exhibit. Or they carve your company's name out of one of the panels, and light it from behind, like a Halloween pumpkin. In the second example, they would affix colored gel, a common photographer's tool, to the back of the panel, creating a tinted effect. The operative phrase is, "exhibit producer crafts." This is a graphical technique exhibit producers excel at.

Exhibit graphics

Of course, all the signs and graphics we talk about here are "exhibit" graphics. But there is a class of graphics that is designed, produced and incorporated into the exhibit. Perhaps a poster-like graphic is printed and then mounted onto one of the exhibit's panels. Or it's printed onto a piece of clear film, mounted onto the exhibit panel and lighted from behind. The effect is dramatic.

A popular way to use exhibit graphics is to print a large, specially designed graphic onto a thin, flexible piece of plastic and attach it to a pop-up-style backwall. The graphic can be, and usually is, large enough to cover the entire exhibit. The really neat thing is that it attaches with simple Velcro. The other really neat thing is, it rolls up like a poster, making it easy to carry.

The key word here is "printed onto". Exhibit graphics are printed directly onto a medium. That product is then Velcro-ed onto, mounted or otherwise attached to the exhibit.

Signs

"For Sale" and "Eat at Joe's", are examples of signs. Instead of metal backing, trade show signs are mounted on a lighter-weight material. Plexiglas, cardboard with a foam center-these are the types of materials used. Signs describe or illustrate a product, make an announcement or add a message to your exhibit. They are the most likely items that will change from show to show.

There are two ways to create a sign: print or appliqué. In the first method, a graphic or sign is printed as a poster, and mounted on special cardboard. In the second method, letters, symbols, even corporate logos are machine-cut from vinyl sheets, and applied to Plexiglas or special cardboard.

Hanging signs

A great way to call attention to your exhibit is to hang a sign from the ceiling above your booth. A person standing at the entrance can see a sign hanging in the rear of the hall.

Hanging signs are usually reserved for larger exhibits, 400-square-feet or more. Convention center ceilings rise 20 feet above the hall floor. Regulations on sign height and size may vary from facility to facility. Trade show management provides exhibitors with diagrams of the show floor, and a list of specifications and limitations for exhibits and hanging signs.

Though they take on different shapes and colors, their functions are the same: they beckon people to the exhibit. So, no matter what their form, all hanging signs contain the company's logo and/or its name. They may also show the company tag line (its motto, or statement of the company's goals), if it is short enough.

Hanging signs are made of either vinyl or nylon. Since the sign must be fairly light, nylon is the usual choice. Letters and logos are made from vinyl and applied to the sign. You can also use nylon letters and logos, which are stitched onto the sign. This is much more expensive, but it lasts a lot longer than vinyl appliqué.

Does this sound familiar? It should. Some of the same techniques used in standard stiff-backed signs, described in the section above, "apply" here. The same folks who make appliqué-style signs also make hanging signs. Same technique, same technology—with one key difference. The sign simply needs to be propped up, and it's ready to use. The hanging sign has to have a frame to fit onto so that it can hang from the hall ceiling.

Who Do You Hire

If you look at it from another perspective, the practical, procurement point of view, there are three sources for your trade show graphics and signs.

Graphic Artist and Photographer

Here's an obvious set of important sources. If your exhibit is small and simple, you can do most of the creative work yourself—*if* you know how to use graphics software. But once you get into using photographs, colors, and illustrations you need an experienced graphic artist.

If you are working with an exhibit producer, remember that planning and designing a new exhibit is a different sort of artistic endeavor. It's more like architectural design and interior decorating than graphical art. Some exhibit houses have graphics artists on staff, but many do not. So if your exhibit incorporates any kind of graphical images, posters or colorful signage, be sure to have your pro on hand.

The graphic artist works closely with a photographer to create whatever images your graphics require. In this way, the process is no different from planning and designing the cover of a new brochure.

Reprographics

That's "repros" for reproduction, and graphics for...well, graphics. About a thousand years ago, architects and engineers needed a way to make duplicates of their blue prints. These scientists spent weeks drawing their plans by hand. The end result was a set of large renderings, often the size of a desktop. It was necessary to make duplicates, time consuming job.

So the architects and engineers hired other companies to reproduce their blue prints, while they went on with their work of designing buildings and machines.

Through the years, bigger and better machines were created to make bigger and better copies. Along came color capable equipment, and eventually new things to use them for—including exhibit graphics.

Don't mistake reprographics for offset printers, who produce your brochures and data sheets. Yes, reprographics can produce mass quantities of posters just like offset printers. But the technology and equipment are different. Reprographics companies are specialists in high quality digital output for display and presentation purposes. Printers are specialists in high quantity marketing materials like brochures, direct mail post cards, even booklets and manuals.

Here's how it works: you or your graphic artist creates a graphic or sign, using common graphical software. Adobe® Photoshop® or Illustrator®, and QuarkXPress® are popular applications. Macintosh and Quark products dominate the graphics industry, but most reprographics companies work with a variety of formats.

If the graphic requires a photograph or two, you or your artist works with the photographer to create just the right shot. The shot is scanned and converted to digital format, and incorporated into the Adobe® or Quark® file.

Once the design is complete, you or your graphic artist sends the electronic file to the reprographics folks. They copy the file onto their own hard drive. Depending on how you plan to use the sign or graphic, the reprographic folks print out the file to the appropriate media.

Frontlit graphics panel. Current large format output printers can produce paper prints up to 4' x 8' in size. The quality and resolution are amazing. Prices for that 4' x 8' start at about $500.

The paper printout is mounted on a flexible stiff-backed material such as Lexan or Sintra. A clear laminate is applied to protect the print. The display is ready to ship off to the exhibit producer's facility where it is incorporated into the exhibit. Graphics should be updated at least once a year.

The new graphic panel may or may not have its own lighting. We call it "frontlit" to differentiate it from "backlit" graphics.

Backlit graphics panel. The same large format printers can output the file to film media. Instead of paper, the artwork is printed onto a transparent film, usually Kodak Duratrans®. The film is mounted to a thin, transparent backing and shipped off to the exhibit producer.

The new graphic is framed and incorporated into the exhibit. What makes this a standout display is the special lamp set inside the panel, illuminating the Duratrans® print from behind.

Graphics sign. This stand-alone display can be as small as a sheet of note paper or as large as a basketball player. Your electronic file is printed onto paper.

The sign can be creative artwork, standard text or a combination. It is mounted onto a special cardboard-foam core backboard. For a little more money, you can have your sign mounted on sturdier stock made of PVC. The sign is covered with a clear protective laminate.

All you need now is something to prop up your sign. An easel back (like the ones propping up the framed photos on your dresser) works well for small signs. Use easel stands (artist and presentation-type stands) for larger signs.

Banners. Reprographics companies now have the technology to print signs and graphics on banner material. Your logo, text, photographs, even the same type of artwork you put on your brochures can go on a banner you hang in your exhibit.

Sign and Banner Makers

You've seen their work. The "Coming Soon" sign for the new coffee shop opening at the mall next month. The logo and message on the doors of your plumber's pick-up truck. The Realtor's "For Sale" sign outside the house down the street. That's what they do, that's what they've always done.

The first sign makers painted letters and numbers on doors, windows and posters to create the message. Later, alphanumerics were cut from sheets of vinyl and applied to the surface. Vinyl appliqué is still used today.

Practically everyone has a message to send, and sign makers are happy to help. If you want to prop it in front of your business or hang it from the roof, they will find a way to do it. Here's what sign and banner makers can do for you:

Vinyl appliqué on acrylic. This one has been around for years, and remains popular. Acrylic is a sort of plastic. You may be more familiar with its common trade name, Plexiglas™. It is made in a variety of colors and is ideal for vinyl appliqué. Many sign makers still apply vinyl by hand. But computer software and sophisticated machinery let the sign maker create elaborate logos, symbols and alphanumeric figures. The great thing about acrylic signs is that the backboard can be used over and over. What makes this a less attractive option is that the old vinyl is removed by hand, which takes a long time.

Acrylic signs come in all sizes. However, larger signs are heavy and hard to transport. Keep that in mind when planning your signs.

Vinyl appliqué on nylon banner. If you believe in perfection, nylon is the perfect material for indoor exhibits. Most hanging signs—displays suspended above exhibits—are made of nylon. It's a versatile, sturdy material. Nylon gym bags, wind breakers and Frosty the Snowman flags are some examples.

Here's how it works: You or your graphic artist creates a design for a banner using popular graphics software. It will be a relatively simple affair, letters, numbers, logos, whatever can be cut from a sheet of vinyl appliqué. You hand over the electronic file containing the banner art to your sign maker.

You tell them what type and color banner material to use. You tell them how large to make it, and how you plan to use your banner, so the sign people can give it the proper finish. Maybe you will have the edges sewn over so that a length of PVC pipe can slide through. Maybe you will have grommets, metal eyelet that protect a hole in the fabric, added so that you can use rope to hang the banner.

The sign people prepare the proper size of banner material. They load your art file into their computer and prepare the vinyl lettering, numbers and symbols just as they do for acrylic signs. The vinyl lettering is applied to the banner material.

Banners can last a long time, and work best for messages that rarely change. Two things to remember. First, put some care and thought into packing and storing your banner. If you fold and store it for long periods of time, the vinyl appliqué starts to crack and wear along the folds. Try rolling it up and storing it like a rug.

Second, the vinyl appliqué on banners is permanent. Once it's done, it's done. You can't peel it off and reuse the banner.

Vinyl appliqué on vinyl banner. The most durable banner material used, vinyl, is available in a variety of colors. It also comes in several different thicknesses and is great for outdoor displays. Creating and applying letters and symbols to vinyl is the same as applying them to acrylic.

As different as they look, the technique for producing the two types of banner is identical. Nylon is light, fresh and trendy. Vinyl banners are heavy and solid and more suited for outdoor events.

Digital imaging on nylon. This is a costlier option and it is worth it, if you have the budget. The end product is more attractive than vinyl appliqué. Large format digital imaging equipment uses a technique called dye sublimation to transfer your graphics onto the nylon banner. Any graphic you care to create—photographs, advertisements, brochure covers—is transferred onto the fabric; something vinyl appliqué cannot provide.

Hanging signs. Mount a banner on a lightweight frame, suspend it from the ceiling above your exhibit, and you have a hanging sign. It's a little more complicated than that, but only a little.

Hanging signs can take a variety of shapes. The most common start with a rectangular piece of nylon banner.

- •Single sided. One piece of nylon banner with graphics on a single side, mounted in a lightweight frame.
- •Double sided. One piece of vinyl banner, with graphics on two sides, mounted in a lightweight frame.
- •Three sided. Three pieces of nylon banner with graphics on one side of each piece, mounted in a lightweight frame to form a triangle.
- •Four sided. Four pieces of nylon banner with graphics on one side of each piece, mounted in a lightweight frame to form a square.
- •Circular. A single piece of nylon banner with graphics on one side, mounted in a lightweight frame to form a circle.

Hanging signs are a great way to lead attendees to your exhibit because the are visible from every corner of the convention floor and they make a lasting impression. Simple signs are easy to design. But the snag is the frame. Not all sign makers are equipped to make them. And those who are, may not specialize in hanging signs for trade shows. Those who do not make the frame may be the best-darned sign makers in town. What to do?

You have three options. First, you can find a sign maker who can both reproduce your sign and construct the frame.

Or you can have your exhibit crafter build the frame, while your sign maker creates the sign. The advantage here is that your exhibit crafter, with all his knowledge of convention center rules and regulations, helps you design the hanging sign.

Lastly, you can hire a company that specializes in creating hanging signs for trade show exhibitors. Specialists may be more expensive, but they have all the latest equipment and materials. They also have the artistic vision to take you beyond the designs described above.

But no matter who you choose to create your hanging sign, remember one thing: the final product must meet common convention center regulations, with respect to the rest of your exhibit's height.

Banners: Who to Hire

Advances in technology now let sign makers print artwork directly onto banner material. Sound familiar? There's a minor convergence in services as sign makers and reprographics companies use the same equipment to offer the same product to their customers. But while there may be some overlap, these two vendors are really quite different.

Reprographics companies have relied on advanced technology for a long time. Large format printing, digital imaging, scanning and copying are the core of their business. The technology of reproducing images is new to sign makers. They've relied on machines that cut computer-generated letters and images from vinyl sheets.

On the other hand, sign makers have been hanging signs and banners for years. Printing art onto banner material is one thing. Preparing the banner to hang is another. There are a few low-tech steps, and that's one of the sign maker's core skills.

So, whom do you choose to make your banner? To answer that question, you'll need to do a little research. First, write down your banner's specifications. Next, answer these questions:

•Does your reprographics company do banners?

•Does your sign maker have the equipment to print your photographic banner? Can they work to your specifications?

•Does your reprographics company or sign maker have experience making the kind of banner you need?
•How much do they charge for producing the banner?

Cheat Sheet

To organize a trade show, it may feel like you have to be an expert in everything. But it only seems that way. The trick to creating great graphics is to find the experts and hire *them* to do the work. The trick to working with the experts is knowing where to find them, deciding which ones to hire and managing them effectively.

Here's what we learned in this chapter:

•There are four types of graphics used in trade show exhibits:
   Structural—something that is a physical part of the exhibit structure.
   Exhibit—a sign or graphic incorporated into the exhibit.
   Signs—posters, placards.
•Hanging signs—suspended above from the ceiling above the booth.
•From the manager's point of view, there are three types of service providers of graphics:
   Graphic artists and photographers
   Reprographics companies
   Sign and banner makers
•Both sign makers and reprographics companies can help you with signs, banners and hanging signs. Who you choose depends on your budget and requirements and the qualifications of the vendor.

Part 2 - Fist Full of Leads: Seducing Great Prospects

Calling All Prospects: How to Use Advertising and Public Relations to Maximize Your Trade Show Success

What if you threw a party and no one showed up? Think about it. You hired a caterer and a band, you have enough paté and champagne for 200. Valet parking, the good crystal, and there you sit. You and your mate in your expensive new clothes, alone, but no guests, not even a last minute phone call with "Oh I'm sorry we can't make it." You spent a fortune on an empty room.

Did a freak storm wash out the roads? Are your friends rude, every last one of them?

It's really quite simple. You didn't send out invitations. You didn't even make out a guest list. You just figured that if you catered a swanky affair, during "high season", all the right people would know. They would show up, and be impressed, and…

How ridiculous is that? You would never give a party without a guest list, without invitations and RSVPs? Yet that is what many trade show exhibitors do. They rent booth space, send their exhibit and staff, hoping to scoop up hundreds of leads. But they don't invite anyone. They don't tell anyone "Hey, we're exhibiting at XYZ Expo—come and see our new voice activated telephone." They figure that out of the twenty thousand or so people predicted to attend, they'll pull in more than enough leads.

But trade shows don't work that way. If you don't promote yourself well before the show, you rely on the strength of your exhibit to attract prospects. Remember that your exhibit competes with dozens or hundreds of others, some more captivating than your own. Most of your leads will be attendees who just happened to walk by your exhibit.

Promoting your company *before* the show increases the quality and number of leads you pull in *at* the show. By advertising, direct mail and media coverage, you let potential customers know that you are exhibiting. The more you put into the effort, the more high-quality leads you'll take home after the show.

"More" doesn't necessarily mean more expensive or more work. It means a thorough, well thought out campaign with professionally designed ads, direct mail and news releases.

Here's what a successful, conservative campaign might look like. Joe Prospect, supply chain manager at Major Distributor Inc., sits in his office, drinking his morning coffee and reading his favorite business journal. A snappy advertisement catches his eye. *YourCo*, Inc. has a new line of voice-activated telecommunications products. Interesting. Oh, and they're exhibiting at XYZ Expo next month. "Hey, he syas, "didn't I read something about that in last month's "Technical Journal"?

Fast-forward two weeks. Joe sits at his desk, eating lunch and going through his mail. His assistant has pre-sorted the pile, tossing the obvious junk mail. But among the correspondence is a provocative direct mail piece. It's from *YourCo*. There are two complimentary guest passes to the exhibit floor enclosed. He's been looking forward to the trade show all year. Joe reads the letter that came with the passes. He saves the letter in his "Must See at XYZ" folder, and notices a postcard-sized mailer from *YourCo* that he'd tossed in last week.

"Time to make plans" Joe thinks to himself. He digs into the folder, reviewing all the notes and direct mail he's received during the last month. Not all of them make the cut. In fact, Joe ends up throwing out more than half. But *YourCo* makes it onto the list. The ad, the article, the mailer and the post card have lodged your company in Joe's brain. Besides, that new telecommunications product is something he really ought to see. If it does everything that the Technical Journal article says it does, it would fill the gap in Major Distributor's product line.

Joe finishes filling out his dance card, the list of exhibits he wants to visit. It's a long one. There are a several companies he's never heard of, like *YourCo*. There are also many major manufacturers on the list. Industry leaders, exhibits Joe would want to see with or without direct mail or complementary guest passes.

Fast forward again. Joe meets with his boss, the division's vice president, one last time before they both depart for the trade show. The VP waves a colorful post card at Joe.

"Make sure we go by *YourCo*'s exhibit, will ya?" The VP had never before mentioned *YourCo* to Joe, never hinted that she'd heard of them. In fact, though she browsed the same magazines and received the same direct mail as Joe, it was that second post card that finally caught her attention.

You see, as head of an entire division, the VP must read more magazines and technical journals, sift through lots more information than Joe does. The VP has a lot more competing for her attention.

Determine Your Objectives

YourCo put together a media campaign that successfully boosted the number of leads captured during the trade show. Even better, the percentage of strong prospects was up from the last time they exhibited at XYZ Expo.

A campaign needn't be complicated. It can draw from the basic marketing disciplines; public relations, advertising and direct mail. Planning the campaign doesn't have to be painful either. It's as simple as knowing your objectives and choosing your weapons.

YourCo exhibited at XYZ Expo to expand the public's awareness about the company and grow the customer base. Its main goal at the show was to increase the number of qualified leads. Because *YourCo* is a small company and not well known, management knew they needed something specific to draw the attention of attendees.

The new voice-activated telephone would be ready in time for the show. A "new product launch" would make a strong theme. So, with a few modifications to the PR and advertising programs, and a few extra direct mail pieces, *YourCo* had a successful campaign.

Using PR

There is no better advertisement than a feature article about the company in an industry technical journal. Or news item. Even a short paragraph in a round-up piece has more credibility than a big, eye-catching advertisement. We tend to believe what we read in the newspaper, technical journals and magazines.

After all, the publisher *chose* to write about the company or the product. No one paid them to do it. That's the theory, anyway. And though not all publications have a strict separation between editorial and advertising, content has the ring of gospel.

That's the good news. The bad news is that getting into print takes a lot of time and effort. It's not enough to tell an editor about your hot new product. You have to convince him that it's one of *the* hottest new products, and that he'll enthrall his readers by writing about it. Here's where PR agencies help.

A news release helps you get your foot in the door. If a release is professionally presented with pre-printed envelope and letterhead, in standard news release format, the editor may read the headline. If the release is well written, he may read the first paragraph. If the first paragraph has compelling information, he may read the rest of the release.

If the rest of the release is interesting, or if the company is well known, or the editor is writing a feature story on a similar product or company, or...any number of reasons, he will place the release with dozens of others just like it. Otherwise, it becomes a few sheets of recycled paper.

Public relations, of course, is more than writing a great news release and sending it to the editors. No matter who handles the trade show PR, agency or marketing department, you need to know about these important tools.

Pre-Show News Release

Start generating interest early. If you are introducing a new product or service at the trade show, send your press release at least two months before the event. Don't assume that editors of a magazine associated with the show also work on the show dailies. This isn't always the case, so be sure to send releases to both publications.

Press Conference

If your company's big news is fresh, and truly BIG, consider holding a press conference during the event. Editors attend trade shows looking for new products, industry trends and quotes for their stories. A press conference is an editor's chance to hear the announcement in person, and to ask follow-up questions while the news is still fresh in his mind.

A few rules to remember: Send invitations to specific editors and reporters. Invite them early, at least a few weeks ahead of time. Have a senior company official, preferably the president or vice president of your company, give the presentation. Editors, like everyone else, want to go straight to the top corporate officials.

Make it brief. Editors and reporters have a lot of ground to cover at trade shows and they'll appreciate your consideration of their valuable time. Rehearse your presenter, and make sure he or she is well prepared.

Try to plan your conference so that it does not conflict with other conferences and events. Trade shows are notoriously noisy, so, set aside a quiet corner of the exhibit for your conference. Have enough press kits available. Follow up with each editor and reporter after the show.

One-On-One Meetings

Often, press conferences are not an option. Another great way to get in front of editors and reporters is through individual meetings. Again, start early. Contact members of the press at least several weeks before the show.

The best times to meet are during the first day of the event, particularly the first few hours. You may find yourself being stood up for later meetings. But, and this is a big but, never, never ditch an editor or reporter. Always be available for the meeting, even if the other guy is late. Be well prepared, and if possible, bring your president or vice president with you. Always follow up with the editor or reporter after the show.

The Planted Article

It bears repeating, there is no better advertisement than a well-placed feature article. News releases are designed to convince editors to write about your company or product.

An even better ploy is to write the article *for* them. You "pitch" an article idea to the editor, just like a freelance journalist. This works best with certain types of publications—ones that accept freelance contributions. Did your chief engineer find a clever solution to a pesky problem? A technical journal may want to tell their readers all about it.

Another idea: a business-to-business publication where your technical services director describes how he solved a technical problem for a customer. Yet another: an art-of-business magazine where the chief executive of your company opines on the future of the technology.

Of course, the trick is selling the publication on your story idea. Start early. Remember, most editorial calendars are set at least six months before publication.

The Show-Site Press Kit

All trade shows set aside a room for the press. It's a place where editors can relax and regroup. It's also a place where they can find out more about exhibitors. Some editors like to walk the show floor, and then go to the pressroom to pick up kits. Others start in the pressroom, perusing press kits, deciding which exhibits hold the most promise. Count on planting at least 25 kits.

The ideal press kit starts with a basic two-pocket folder. The folder doesn't have to be an elaborate work of art. But it must at least have your corporate logo on the front, and contact information inside.

The kit should include your trade show news release—the one datelined the show's opening day, introducing your new product, service, or other exciting news. Support the release with a product photo. A 5" x 7" or 8" x 10" print will do. But a 35mm slide works better, especially if it contains a lot of color. Photos should be captioned. For prints, type the caption on a pressure sensitive label and affix it to the back of the photo.

Also include a copy of your planted article. If you've received any press coverage during the past eight or so months, include a reproduction of the published article and news items. You can also use one or two of your other, most recent news releases. Always put a copy of the most recent corporate backgrounder in your kit. Top it off with the media contact's business card. Make that two: one for the editor to keep and one for him to share.

Here are a few "do-nots" and "try-nots" for press kits:

•Do not overload the kit with lots of extraneous information. It's a waste of paper and a major turn-off for editors.
•Do not staple or clip individual releases and articles together. Do not write *on* photographs.
•Try not to put in a lot of data brochures or ad reprints. Editors are interested in facts, not fluff.
•Try line cards—a list and brief description of the product lines— and data sheets instead.

On-Line Press Rooms

Also known as "virtual pressrooms". What the electronic version lacks in cachet it makes up for with immediacy and influence. For a fee, your press kit is made available to the media via show management's web site. The service provider uploads your press kit to the site several weeks before the show. Interested editors can download your releases, reprints, and even ready-to-use photos. The one drawback is that you are usually limited to five or six items, including photographs.

The "Best of Show" Award

Most trade shows award a prize to the new product that meets certain criteria, or in some way stands apart from the rest. Sometimes the criterion is advertising in the sponsor's magazine. Either way, winners receive a plaque and electronic art to include in their advertisements and brochures. They also receive a write-up in the sponsor's magazine. All you have to do is tell the contest sponsors that you want them to consider your hot new product.

Advertising

If a feature article about your company is the best form of advertisement, then paid advertisements are the best way to get your message across. Much planning and work go into getting a magazine or journal to write about your products and company. You have to rely on the editor to decide what is newsworthy. Ultimately, you have no control over what he writes. What you *do* have control over are your advertisements.

Where news releases are written like news, ads are written in marketing-speak. Forget the "just the facts, ma'am", inverted pyramid style. Ads are creative and colorful. They let you emphasize the product's strong points and ignore its weaknesses. Your message, your way, and the magazine must print it, because it is your company's money.

There are several ways to use print advertisements in your attempt to lure trade show attendees. The simplest is to start with your current ad campaign.

Putting the Word into Existing Ads

This is the easiest thing in the world to do. Simply pick up the phone and call each magazine where your ads appear. Most are happy to add a few lines of type, even a trade show logo to existing artwork.

"See us at XYZ Expo, November 5-8, 2002, Kalamazoo, MI. Booth 333." Most shows have their own logo, and provide several different electronic and print formats.

Of course, *you* need to decide where the line and logo should appear in your ad. You need to specify the typeface and size. If the ad is well designed, finding the right spot (usually towards the bottom, beneath the copy,) is easy. If the ad is badly designed—completely filled with copy and graphics-you may have to create a new layout.

The best way to handle the "change order" is to print a copy of the ad's artwork (a laser printer copy) with the new line and logo in place. Attach a note with the change request, specifications and directions. Fax the copy to the magazine's production office, but only after calling in with your request.

Three more tips. Make your change request before the magazine's deadline for new material. Next, consider adding the line and show logo to all the publications in which the ad appears. And finally, know that you don't have to limit it to the month of the trade show. It's okay to advertise one or two months prior to the event.

Advertising in the Show Guide

The trade show guide is the booklet of exhibitor listings handed to every attendee as they enter the convention center. It lists every exhibit in detail. The show guide contains company contact names, telephone numbers, web addresses and e-mail addresses. It is the "who's who" and "what's what" of your industry. Buyers, specifiers and decision-makers hold onto the guides for at least a year. Show guides outlive magazines, advertising in them is always a great idea.

Many advertisers use their existing ads, scaled down to fit the smaller guide format. Others use the same design concept, but alter the photos and content.

Opportunities Through the Internet

While the Internet hasn't revolutionized the trade show industry (yet), it has added many new avenues of promotion for exhibitors.

Virtual exhibits. The Internet is hard-pressed to take the place of trade shows, but many sponsors are adding virtual exhibits to the live-action event. It is a new concept.

Currently, virtual exhibits are still little more than elaborate on-line brochures. Like the virtual press office, on-line exhibits are "set-up" days or weeks before the event, and taken down after the physical exhibits are long gone. They offer attendees a way to preview the exhibits before leaving the office and review them after returning from the show.

Hot link from show management's web site. Most trade shows maintain a site devoted to the show. Many show sponsors are associated with a magazine or publisher of several magazines, and most sponsor more than one event. All trade show web sites eventually post a list of exhibitors, often several months before the event. For a fee, you can arrange for your listing to be hot linked to your company's web page.

Other Show-Site Advertising Opportunities

Alternative advertising ideas are diverse, and vary from show to show. They all come under the heading of "Sponsorships". For a fee, often a very big fee, your company's name and logo are splashed over some aspect of the exhibit hall. Some sponsorships are exclusive, meaning, you alone have the privilege. Others are opportunities that are shared with a few other sponsors. Here is a list and brief description of the most popular on-site opportunities.

Press Room. Sponsor the press corps's hangout and have your name and logo in front of them during the entire event.

Badge Holder Insert. The badge holder is a clear plastic piece that holds the name badge of everyone who enters the exhibit hall. For your sponsorship, you get an attractive insert with the company name and logo, in every badge holder.

Lanyard advertising. A shoelace-like lanyard clipped to the badge holder hangs around the attendee's and exhibitor's neck. For a fee, your company's name and logo is printed onto every lanyard.

Badge mailer. Most people register well before the event. These organized individuals receive their badges early, through the US Postal Service. Sponsor the mailer and your company's name and logo appears on the envelope or on a direct mail piece included with the badge.

Official Show Bag. Everyone, attendees and exhibitors, receive an official show bag when they first enter the exhibit hall. Your money buys ad space on the fabric or plastic bag.

Concession Area Cups/Napkins. Your company's name and logo, printed on paper cups and napkins.

Executive breakfasts and luncheons. Most trade shows host dual function get-togethers for executive attendees. As a sponsor, your company name and logo are prominently displayed to decision-makers and specifiers for several hours, while they network and enjoy a meal.

Shuttle Buses. Many trade shows offer shuttle buses to ferry attendees from hotel to exhibit hall. Your advertisement on the bus's side spreads your message around town.

Aisle Signs. You are never lost on the crazy, crowded trade show floor. Just look up. Aisle signs hanging from the ceiling let you know where you are. Some events sell advertising space on aisle signs.

Internet Café. Many trade shows now set up an area where people can retrieve their e-mail and stay in touch with their office. Your sponsorship dollars put your company name and logo in front of e-mail retrieving web surfing attendees.

Direct Mail

It is an art form, the old standby. It is easy to do, too. Direct mail. But the average target of direct mail ends up filing most of it in the small round file cabinet on the floor, next to his desk. Unread.

However direct mail does the job if executed properly. That means creating a great message, adding eye-catching graphics and putting it on a wonderful medium (post card, clever sales letter in a clever envelope.) It means sending your direct mail to people most likely to pay attention. An art form.

Direct mail is used to promote your exhibit before the show and to promote your exhibit *after* the show. Most shows make available for rent, both pre-and post-show attendee lists. Here are some simple ways you can boost your trade show success.

Post Cards

Inexpensive and simple, post cards are a great way to promote your company's exhibit. They needn't cost a lot to create. Two or three colors, a few lines of clever copy, your logo and the trade show's logo will do it.

Direct mail is like print advertising. The recipient usually needs several imprints, needs to see the ad or post card several times, before the message starts to register. So, ideally, the campaign includes at least two separate mailings of the same card design to each person on your mailing list.

The mailings should be timed carefully, synchronized with the trade show's calendar. Many exhibitors time their first mailer to arrive four weeks before the show, and their second mailer to arrive one or two weeks before opening day.

Sending Complimentary Guest Passes

As an exhibitor, you are entitled to as many free exhibit guest passes as you can use. If you order early, show management will print your company's name on each pass. Endear yourself to your customers and potential prospects by sending free exhibit passes. Always send at least two—one for the recipient and one for him to share with a colleague.

Sales Letters

A letter goes beyond the visual, subliminal message of a post card. It allows you to engage the reader's intellect, to show how your company's product will improve his life. Reading the letter, he goes through a thought process, whether he's aware of it or not.

As an exhibitor, you are not just convincing the reader to buy your product. You are luring him to your trade show exhibit where you can get your hands on him, so to speak. Your letter must show the reader not only that your product fulfills his needs, but that he needs to drop by your exhibit.

Sales letters are fun to write. But if you need to outsource the work, plan to spend a few hundred dollars. Top agencies and freelancers charge a minimum of $1,000 per page. Here are a few general rules on the art and craft of sales letters.

Grammar and spelling. Always check, and recheck the letter for correct grammar and spelling.

One page. Limit the letter to one page. Resist the urge to decrease margins so that you can fit more text. The longer the letter, the less likely it is to be read.

Headlines. Feel free to use advertising-style headlines to open your letter.

Typeface. A few italicized and bold-faced words can make the letter more interesting. But don't over-do it.

Trade show logo. The trade show logo helps to dress the letter up, and lend legitimacy to its content.

Guest pass. Combine a sales letter with two guest passes.

Advanced Proselytizing: The Big Schmooze

So, you plan the trade show, herd attendees into your exhibit and come away with hundreds of qualified leads. You croon to yourself, "Is that all there is?" Well all right, trade shows are a lot of work and what you *really* think is "Never again!"

But at some point in her career, every experienced trade show manager asks herself, "How can I get more out of each event?"

How can you use the same event to reach an even wider audience, land more customers, create an industry presence, get more press coverage, and leave a greater impression?

The trade show can work for you long after the event ends. There are several techniques you can use.

In-Booth Giveaways

The easiest and least expensive way to leave a lasting impression is to give attendees a gift. It's the gift that keeps on giving. A coffee cup, mouse pad, CD carrying case, tee-shirt, with your company's name and logo is something the attendee will have for long time. The possibilities are endless.

Giveaways can be more elaborate. A personal planner, an athletic bag, a designer pen set, all with a proviso: sit in on a demonstration, get a nice gift.

You can be clever about it, too. Win a free electronic organizer—give us your business card, and we'll give you a raffle ticket.

Before committing to a giveaway program, check the convention center regulations and local laws and ordinances. Some marketing techniques, such as raffle tickets, may be against the rules or even the law.

Mini-Conference Room

Create an area within the booth where salespeople can talk one-on-one with attendees. Perhaps a longtime customer drops by, a hot prospect expresses great interest or an important editor has questions. Having a conference room built into the exhibit gives you a nice, quiet, some might say "controlled" environment for meetings and presentations.

The room can be as simple as a table and chairs. Walls add a sense of privacy that lets you focus on your audience. Large exhibitors have the luxury of a more spacious meeting room. But any exhibitor can enhance their conference room by arranging for a few snacks.

Hospitality Suites

If you are ready to take a big step up from an in-booth conference room, rent a hotel suite. The best spot for a hospitality suite is the event's primary hotel, where most of the attendees stay. If the trade show takes place in a hotel ballroom, use a suite in the same building.

Suites bring you face-to-face with specific customers and prospects where you can give more elaborate presentations. The experience is a more satisfying one that demonstrates to your audience that you hold them in high regard. Your company also comes across as an established, solid organization.

Of course, catering is a must—coffee and sandwiches at a minimum. And though hospitality suites are not inexpensive, they are the closest things to an exclusive presentation. If planned well, they can help your salespeople close a few deals.

There's the rub: "Well planned" doesn't mean simply renting a room and ordering room service.

Make appointments. Invite a specific prospect or client. Several weeks before the show, call or write the person or group. Arrange the meeting for a specific time.

Don't over_lap_. Make sure no one overbooks the suite. You don't want your customers and prospects running into one another, especially if they are competitors.

Keep it clean. Make sure the suite is clean, well stocked and ready for service at all times. A stale smell and used cocktail napkins make you look stale and used. The same applies to the suite's facilities. Make sure the bathroom is neat and clean at all times. Bring in fresh towels and a deodorizer if you have to. Negative impressions last longer than positive ones.

Don't overdo it. The idea is to make it a pleasant experience for your guest. _You_ know that the meeting is arranged so your salespeople can pitch the product, perhaps close a sale. You know it, and your guest knows it. But don't overwhelm them with it. Make your case without making your guest a prisoner.

Use it. Using a hospitality suite to meet with prospects is a great idea. But why limit yourself? How about meetings with established clients to get reacquainted, strengthen relationships? Or a meeting between your CEO and your client's CEO? Or a meeting with editors and reporters in arranged interviews and press conferences

Host a Party or Gathering

Parties, luncheons and dinners are where people network, relax and have fun. How about hosting an event that pulls them in from a variety of organizations. Here are some good reasons.

Networking. While your guests are busy networking, not working and having a good time, your salespeople are busy networking with your guests. They are swapping business cards and picking up leads.

Captive audience. "And now a few words from our sponsor." The company's president, vice president, or other impressive senior officer stands on the podium and delivers a short speech.

Good vibes. Your guests leave with a positive impression of the company. They've had a good time, good food, good drink. They've made new friends, caught up with old friends. They've formed new business associations, perhaps found a better job. And they owe it all to your company.

Hosting special events is not risk free. You must be careful in planning your event. Do your homework, make sure your party or luncheon or dinner does not coincide with another, more popular event.

Cheat Sheet

It's not enough to simply show up at the trade show, put up your exhibit and hope a lot of qualified prospects wander into your booth. You need to let people know ahead of time that you are exhibiting. Seduce them into stopping by your exhibit. Convince editors to write about you in their publications.

This is where marketing expertise comes in handy. Here's what we learned in this chapter:

- Determine your objectives before mapping out a pre-show marketing strategy.

- Use public relations before the show to create interest, and after the show to leave an impression.
- Advertise to let potential customers know you will be exhibiting. Advertise at the show, as well.
- Use the Internet to promote your participation in the event.
- Tap into the many show site marketing and advertising opportunities.
- Direct mail is an inexpensive way to lure current customers and potential new business.
- Boost leads with advanced techniques such as giveaways, hospitality suites, hosted parties.

The Well Trained Booth Staff

You've been looking forward to this all day. Your favorite television series, a science fiction program about a space vessel and its crew, wanders the galaxy, far from home. The heroes battle the alien enemy-of-the-week. It is ship against ship, crew against crew. The enemy ship fires upon our heroes again and again.

"Captain, shields are down to 80%," the First Officer shouts. "They're ignoring our hails."

"Evasive maneuvers." The captain barks. The enemy is a worthy foe. But ultimately, they are no match for the Captain and her crew.

"Arm photon torpedoes."

"But Captain," the First Officer says, "we didn't bring any!"

The enemy vessel swings around for one final blast. The captain's eyes widen; her jaw drops. The ship explodes into a million tiny pieces. It turns out that for all their sophistication and technology, they didn't pack the weapons.

Exhibiting at a trade show without trained booth staff is like going into battle without your primary weapons. You can have the slickest, most focused and well designed exhibit. You can fill it with great products, snazzy presentations and support it with advertising and public relations. But if you aren't packing great salespeople, you're dead.

Picture this: The exhibit is great, the displays are great and lots of attendees are wandering into the booth. One in particular stands staring at the new self-tying athletic foot apparel display. The exhibitor's top salesman approaches.

"Can I answer any questions?"

"No." And the attendee wanders off to the next exhibit. *Game Over.*

Or this:

"Can I answer any questions?" the salesman asks.

"Yes. How many colors does this come in?" She asks.

"We make these in black, red, mauve and gold." The salesman smiles. Again, *Game Over.*

Why? In both scenes, the salesman asked closed-ended questions, questions that could be answered "yes" or "no". Even when the answer is "yes", the salesman fails to score. He has yet to take control of the transaction.

This may seem obvious to you, since it *is* "Sales 101".

Trade Show Sales—How <u>Not</u> to Do It

Do you recognize any of the following trade show sales duds?

Usurpers

Usurpers are salespeople who post themselves inches away from the product display. Most folks have sense of territory, and some will hesitate to move in on the salesperson's space. Also, many attendees want a little bit of time to examine the display before a salesperson starts in on them.

Feature Creatures

These are salespeople who talk about the product's features and ignore their benefits. The consumer considering your self-tying jogging shoes doesn't care how fast they tie themselves (feature), she wants to hear how much more efficient they will be (benefit). She doesn't care so much about the variety of colors (feature), she wants know how sexy she'll look (benefit) wearing them.

Robots

Salespeople who launch into their spiel without first finding out who their audience is are robots. The attendee standing in front of the display might be another exhibitor researching the competition. He could be a long time company customer or a buyer for a retail chain. He could just be curious, but with no real interest in or authority to buy your shoes.

On-and-Ons

These are salespeople who spend too much time with one attendee. One or the other keeps talking and talking. The more time he spends with one prospect, the fewer leads he takes home. In most cases, ten minutes with each prospect is enough.

The idea is to catch and release, catch and release.

Marshmallows

Marshmallows are salespeople who don't close the encounter with a call to action. Marshmallows are related to On-and-Ons. The salesperson won't get the lead if he doesn't ask for it.

"Why don't I call you next week. I can tell you more about our pricing structure." Or, "I'll send some literature as soon as I get back to the office." Better yet, "I'll have that proposal on your desk by the end of the month!" Exchange business cards, run their attendee badge through the lead-capturing device and send them on their way.

If your booth staff can't identify good prospects and successfully pull in useful leads, your company leaves the show empty handed. Salespeople are a company's most important weapons. Make sure your salespeople are ready for battle by training them and arming them with information.

The Lead Gathering Story

Let's begin by reviewing the process. Gathering leads is like reading a good play. It has a first act, a second act and a third act. But in *this* play, the salesperson gets to be the heroine. The prospect is someone in need of rescue.

Act I. Our heroine/salesperson must first engage the story's other character. And it's a lot like meeting someone new at a party. An attendee stops to look at the exhibit, or one of the displays. Smile. "I love those shoes! Are they comfortable, with all the walking you have to do today?" Or, "Oh, I see by your name badge your with XYZ, Corp. in Fairfax, Virginia. I grew up there. Are you from that area originally?" Smile again. It's genuine, pleasant and non-threatening.

Next, she must identify and qualify the other character. Make sure he needs to be rescued. During the next few minutes, she discovers the following about her potential prospect:

His position. Where is he in his company's chain of command? Is he *a decision-maker*? The salesperson certainly hopes so. Decision-makers decide whose product his company buys, and whose proposal it accepts.

Who is the decision-maker? He's the person with the authority to say, "Yes, we'll buy it." That person may vary from company to company. Typically, larger companies authorize the buyer or the sales manager. Smaller companies and entrepreneurial outfits may limit decision making to the CEO or upper management.

Is he an *influencer*? If so, he gives educated advice to the decision-maker on purchasing decisions. Depending on the company's approach to the buying process, any number of people influence the final decision. He might be head of accounting, one of the design engineers, project manager, sales manager, even one of the folks who end up using your product.

Is he a *specifier*? Specifiers are the folks who tell the decision-maker what type of product the company should buy or what kinds of elements the company should look for in a proposal.

Specifiers are often the people who end up using the product. For example, Mom, Dad and little Johnny are shopping in a department store. Johnny spies a particular toy, the "Mr. Mucho Macho" Urban Commando doll and immediately begs Mom to buy it for him. He lists all the reasons why he needs the doll, why it has to be that particular doll and not a (cheaper) alternative. Johnny is the specifier.

His company's needs. Does the attendee's company need the salesperson's product or services? More importantly, do they need enough of the product to make this worth your salesperson's time? If the company sells laptop computers in mass quantities and the prospect buys for a small, single-location company, she needs to move on. If, on the other hand, the prospect is a product manager for a major computer equipment distributor, the salesperson has a great lead.

Most important of all, does the salesperson's product or service fit in with the prospect's needs? If the distributor only handles office furniture and the prospect needs shoes, it's time to move on.

Buying time. How soon will they need the product or service? Perhaps the prospect is a buyer for a major chain of hospitals with facilities in cities across the nation. The parent company is upgrading the computer networks at each facility and the plan includes several hundred laptop computers for each site. The project is already in full swing, and they plan to purchase within the next six months.

Or, the parent company is studying the feasibility of upgrading their facilities' networks. They may (or may not) purchase within the next year and a half. Still, this is a decent prospect.

So, our heroine/salesperson has developed a rapport with the attendee and has asked enough questions to know whether he is a likely prospect.

If he's not, it's "adios attendee." In a nice way, of course. Remember, that consultant unemployed engineer, personal assistant or recent college graduate may be married to the perfect prospect. He may become one himself. **Always leave him with a great impression**.

If the attendee looks like a good prospect, it's on to the next phase.

Act II. Here, the salesperson talks to the prospect about her product or service. She asks a few more questions, fitting her presentation to this particular prospect. The companies' new laptop fits right in with the hospital chain's plan to upgrade networks. It has all the features, she tells the buyer. She describes the benefits and hints at the after-sale service package.

This is not a full-on sales presentation. The goal is not to sell the *product*. **What the trade show salesperson is selling is a follow-up sales call**. She's looking for the opportunity to make the real sales pitch *after* the show.

The heroine/saleswoman spends three or four minutes giving the prospect a general picture of how the product or service will benefit his company. Once she accomplishes that objective, she moves on to the next phase.

Act III. It's time to tag the prospect and release him back into the trade show. The saleswoman will rescue him next week with a sales call. The process takes only a minute or two. But make no mistake: her technique is critical. She must "close" her prospect, where he agrees to a follow-up meeting or sales call. She disengages and retrieves his lead. The best heroes and heroines make these three steps look like one simple action.

"Well this is great. I'd like to hear more about your company's plan to upgrade the networks. Can I call you next week?" Or, "It sounds like our laptop may fit right in with your company's plan. Let me work up some pricing for you. You'll also need to hear more about our extended warranty. I'll call you next week. When would be a good time?"

Our heroine jots down the last of her notes, borrows the prospect's name badge, and swipes it through the card reader. "It was great meeting you!" She returns the badge. Smile. Hit the reset button and move on to the next attendee.

That's the process in a nutshell. Oh, it's more complicated than that of course. Some might say it is an art form. Much has been written on the subject. See **Appendix B** for a list of great books on sales techniques.

But simply reading up on the subject is not enough. It'll help you understand the lead qualifying process and that's an important first step because it is different from other types of sales transactions. So much must be accomplished in only ten minutes and the goal is different. The "close" is not a signed contract. Rather, it is an agreement to talk or meet at a later date.

Most salespeople who have been in the business for any length of time have worked a trade show. But experience is no guarantee that he or she is an effective trade show salesperson.

Training programs that teach staff how to engage attendees, qualify leads and close the transaction with a commitment to meet at a later date are the best way to make sure your trade show is a success.

Training the Booth Staff

All salespeople benefit from training, even the most talented and experienced. Training does more than teach skills. It brings the sales staff together and creates camaraderie. Training builds teams, enthusiasm and commitment.

There are several ways you can train your booth staff. You can hire a firm or an individual who specializes in sales training. This service might be expensive, but it pays for itself. Think of it as an investment in your company's success.

An alternative is training videos. There are some good products available designed specifically for trade show sales. In fact, it's a good idea to develop a library of sales training videos and audio books. Check **Appendix A** for resources.

But nothing takes the place of a live, in-person workshop, especially when it is designed for your company. You can develop and administer your own program, or you can boost your workshop with off-the-shelf training videos.

Here is how you might structure your workshop:

Introduction

All great programs begin by motivating the participants. "Why are you here?" the program leader might ask. "Why are you in this job at this particular company, this seminar? What are your goals?"

He makes it personal for each participant. He helps them visualize a specific and desired outcome while energizing the audience. Then he tells the audience exactly what they are going to learn in the course of the workshop.

Lecture

The second component is a description of what trade show sales are and are not. The program leader talks about the process of engaging, qualifying and closing the prospect. He talks about how to pre-identify the prospect before approaching him. He goes through everything the salesperson needs to know and everything he or she needs to do in order to get the lead.

Know your goals. Goal setting is like planning a trip. If you don't know where you are going, you'll never arrive at your destination. Encourage the booth staff to set clear, specific goals.

Some examples are, "I will qualify and gather at least 10 leads every hour that I work the booth."

"By the end of the show, I will have gathered 100 leads, not counting multiple leads from the same company or division. X percent of these leads will be decision-makers and X percent will be high level specifiers.

Know the perfect prospect's profile. Better yet, break your prospects into four categories. "A" list prospects are the most important. "B" list are the second most important. "C" lists are the least critical. "D" listers are not prospects at all.

For example, your "A" list might be made up of corporate decision-makers who plan to purchase within the next six months. They hold a certain position within their company. Define which job titles the "A" listers hold, what type of company they work for. Be as specific as you can. Your "B" list could be specifiers and your "C" list influencers.

Know how to qualify the prospect. Now that you have a good picture of your prospect, you must separate the "A"s from the "B"s, "C"s and "D"s. You need to get to know the prospect and you do this by asking questions. Prepare a list ahead of time. Memorize the list and rehearse.

Understand body language. Reading the prospect's body language is the next best thing to reading his mind. If the prospect shifts his weight and looks away, you know he is losing interest. You change directions, ask an important question and draw him back in again. Spend some time discovering and discussing these unconscious signals.

Know how to close the prospect and retrieve the lead. We talked about this earlier in the chapter. Closing and retrieving takes the least amount of time, but it is the most important part of the encounter. Write out a few scripts and memorize them. Rehearse, but remember to be flexible. It's important to be able to adapt your scripts to each situation.

Know all the important information about your company. Be prepared to answer any and all questions the prospect might ask. Know who the company's officers are, its history, PR news (good and bad), products, services, satellite offices, who to talk to get the latest earnings report. You might find yourself talking to an editor from the Wall Street Journal.

Know all the benefits of your product or service. A feature is the shoelace that ties itself. The benefit is convenience. Expand on that. The self-tying sport shoe saves time for the busy lunch time jogger. It impresses other joggers. Memorize the features and understand their benefits.

Know your competitors and their products or services. "But BigShoe Corp. makes a self-tying sport shoe, and they're less expensive." How do you counter this objection? You know your competition manufactures their product overseas and that the factory's working conditions have been criticized in the press. You know that your competitor's product takes 30 seconds to tie itself—20 seconds longer than *your* self-tying shoe.

Use your knowledge to overcome objections and set your product above the rest.

Know how to demonstrate your product. Describing the product is one thing. But letting the prospective customers experience it for themselves builds excitement. More than that, it lets them see how easy the product is to use. But you need to know how to operate the product. Make it look easy.

Put it all together. End the lecture portion of the workshop by recapping all of the tips and techniques you've taught. Describe the lead gathering process, from engaging the prospect, qualifying him, agreeing to a follow up meeting or phone call and recording their company information. Show how everything you've discussed helps the salesperson qualify the lead.

Describe one or two typical transactions and immediately shift into the next section of the workshop.

Demonstration

Help the salespeople visualize the lead gathering process by demonstrating a transaction from beginning to end. Here is where it helps to have an experienced trade show salesperson or sales trainer. You'll need a volunteer from the audience, someone willing to "play" the prospect.

The demonstration portion of the workshop can be one or two simple examples of engaging, qualifying and closing the prospect. If you want to be more aggressive, write out a few prospect profiles for your volunteers to follow. One might be a specific decision-maker who is shopping around for a new supplier.

Or, maybe the decision-maker already has a supplier whom he uses regularly. Now the salesperson has a challenge to overcome.

If you want to be even more aggressive with demonstrations, design several to illustrate different scenarios. You can also demonstrate how *not* to qualify a prospect.

Role Play

Experience is the best teacher. By immediately putting into practice what they've learned, workshop participants will remember more of the techniques and information you've presented. They can get immediate feedback on what they do right, and what they do wrong. They find out not only what it looks like to land a good lead, but also what it *feels* like.

There are three approaches you can take to the practical, hands-on part of the workshop. The idea is to demonstrate techniques and allow workshop participants to practice what they've learned.

One approach is to perform different scenarios, alternately casting workshop participants in the role of trade show salesperson and prospect. The advantage here is that you can utilize the group enthusiasm and build the team concept. The disadvantage is that in larger groups, not everyone has the opportunity to practice and participate.

Another approach is to break the workshop into several smaller groups, role playing and commenting on each other's performance. This way everyone has the opportunity practice technique. You or an experienced sales trainer can float around to different groups, commenting and making sure they stay on track. The disadvantage is that the sales trainer splits his time between groups, diluting his time and energy. The smaller groups may lose the high-level critiquing available with the larger, inclusive group.

The third alternative is a combination of the large group and smaller groups. Role play in the large group first, reinforcing what participants have learned so far, while demonstrating role play. Then break into smaller groups, making sure everyone has a chance to play "Super Trade Show Salesperson".

Ideally, sales training is an ongoing activity. To get the most out of your trade show training, schedule the workshop a few weeks before the show. Schedule a follow-up session a few days before the show opens. The second session is a brief recap of the original workshop.

Arming the Booth Staff

Sales training is the greatest advantage you can give your booth staff. But you can increase that advantage with something else: information. Knowledge is power. Put together an easy-to-use package of reference material.

Features and Benefits of Your Products

This is a data sheet of sorts, based on the company's line card, or a list and description of the company's line of products, usually printed on one or two pages. But, whereas the line card is sales literature, the features and benefits cheat sheet is for the salesperson's eyes only.

For each product or service feature, list as many benefits as possible. Add a line or two of "sound bites", examples of things salespeople can say to their prospects. Leave space for salespeople to be creative.

Features and Benefits of Competitor's Products

Under each "benefit", describe how your product is better or different. The key here is not to criticize the other company or product, but to overcome the prospect's objections to your company or product.

Again, provide a few sound bites and encourage your staff to write their own.

Sample Scripts

Write a few sample scripts. Nothing elaborate, just a few lines for a few specific situations. Give a blurb about the company's history or about a product line or a specific product. The salesperson can memorize these few specific scripts and use them with prospects.

Short-short scripts work best. Anything longer might sound artificial and rehearsed. Again, encourage salespeople to write their own scripts.

Schedule of the Show's Conference Events

Trade shows are often combined with a series of conferences, lectures and speeches. Most run at the same time as the trade show. Let your salespeople know when each event is scheduled. They will be better equipped to understand and gauge the flow of foot traffic. If Bill Gates is delivering a speech on the future of E-Commerce at 1 pm, they'll know that the decision-makers will be out of sight for an hour or so. They can be ready for a higher concentration of specifiers and non-prospects.

Booth Staff Schedule

Include a list of staff, who goes to lunch when, who goes on break at what time, who is scheduled to work the booth during what hours, and so forth. You've already worked out the schedule well before the show. But write it down and give a copy to the entire staff, to avoid confusion.

Rules, Regulations and Instructions

Here is something else you want to work out ahead of time. Who's in charge, how the staff are to conduct themselves, what to do with the lead, etc.. Again, writing these items down and distributing them to the staff will help keep things organized.

Important Phone Numbers and Addresses

Make sure the staff have all the information they may need while away from the office. Don't neglect to include your corporate headquarters' address, phone and fax, and addresses and phone numbers for each division and office. Important names. Remember to include e-mail addresses and the company web address.

Also include the name and phone number, day and evening, of the company trade show fix-it person—the person who can send via an over-night shipping service, an extra set of media kits, track down the lost shipment, solve whatever problems can't be handled at the show site.

"Managing" the Booth Staff

The perfect show, the perfect booth staff. They arrive at the convention center, the sales and technical people, ready to work. Everyone knows what to do. They pitch in to get the exhibit set up, help each other engage great prospects. The show is three or four days of fun and bright lights. But underneath the smiles is a group of dedicated, focused individuals. The booth staff is a team—an All Star team.

So, what sets this team apart from other less successful exhibitors? The first and most important thing is that each knows they are there to work. But it is also important for exhibit staff to relax and smile. A relaxed staff equals happy attendees who want to spend time in your exhibit.

Successful salespeople keeps their eye on the goal. For the company, the goal is more sales. For the salesperson, it might be more sales, or impress the boss, or increase his or her own database of customers.

Successful exhibit staffers know who is in charge during the show. Sometimes, establishing a clear line of authority is a tricky, sticky matter.

Back at the office, Johnny Salesman knows who his boss is, who his colleagues are. He knows the rules and what's expected of him. At the trade show he becomes a part of a different team. Maybe his sales manager stayed home. Suzy Saleswoman, from his own office, is competing for the same promotion. There's a manager from another division, and a sales man from the satellite office in Atlanta, and then there's the marketing manager.

Who is in charge? Smaller companies may have a single sales division, making it an obvious choice. For larger companies, it is more involved.

In either case, the ultimate authority is usually someone other than you. If you are the marketing manager, coordinator, PR agency account representative, anyone other than the most senior sales manager, you won't be the one telling the booth (sales) staff what to do. If problems with the staff come up, like lunch schedule mix-ups or territory conflicts, you usually won't have the authority to solve them.

So, how do you help the booth staff have a successful show when you're not in charge of the salespeople? You need to accomplish three things.

First, you need to turn the staff into a team. If the team isn't working with each other, they are working against one another. This is just as important for small companies where the booth staff is the entire sales team. Selling at trade shows is different from any other kind of sales. For medium and large companies, team building is more critical.

Also, you need to set firm ground rules. As any experienced trade show manager will tell you, the rules must be specific. They cover everything from dress codes and personal hygiene to how the staff treats prospects and how the leads are handled. A sample set of rules is presented at the end of this chapter.

Finally, the staff needs to know who is in charge at the show. Who is going to make sure the lunch schedule works for everyone? Who is responsible for collecting the leads at the end of each day? Who talks to Johnny and Suzie about stealing leads?

The key to accomplishing these three things is interdependence. Whatever position you hold, trade show or marketing manager or agency account representative, you must know who the key sales manager is and create a mutually beneficial relationship.

In a small company, this might be one person—the sales director. In a larger company, there may be several. You will work with the head of each sales division.

The Booth Staff Code of Conduct

Below are guidelines that many exhibitors find helpful. Use them as the basis for your own list of do's and don'ts.

Wear comfortable shoes. Booth staff are on their feet at least four hours every day, for three to five days. Ouch. Be sure to wear shoes with good arch support and cushion, and consider getting a pedicure before opening day.

Wear the company uniform. Establish a dress code, whether it is company-issued sports shirts and khaki pants or business suits. Specify a color scheme for suits, ties, dresses and shoes. Specially designed and supplied company shirts should be dry cleaned to avoid fading.

Wear clean clothes everyday. Everyone needs to take enough clean clothing, including <u>underwear</u>, for each day of the show, plus an extra set. Plus, extra outfits for after-hours socializing and schmoozing.

Bathe every day. Experienced trade show managers will tell you, sadly, to include personal hygiene on your list. More specifically, show up for each booth shift clean and neatly dressed. Good hygiene in this case includes staying sober, and does not include being hung over.

Eat healthy foods and drink plenty of water. Eat a solid breakfast, a light lunch and a good dinner. Eat light snacks throughout the day to keep the energy up. Avoid heavy meals, especially during the day, since these tend to slow the body down. Eat plenty of fruits and vegetables. Humans require up to two quarts of water every day. Dehydration causes fatigue and can make a person more vulnerable to colds and flu.

Don't drink alcohol during the workday. Its tempting, especially when it is served on the show floor. Salespeople want to be sociable with prospects, it makes sense to have a drink with a client. But for many salespeople, one or two drinks are enough to take the edge off their game. For others it is an invitation to disaster.

Avoid drinking during off-show hours. This is tough advice to take. There are a lot of drawbacks to a night of drinking: embarrassing oneself in front of customers, the boss or the press, hangovers, slowed thinking the next day.

Don't drink or eat in the booth. It gives a bad impression and it's messy.

Don't talk on the telephone. If a salesperson is on the telephone, they are unavailable to talk to a prospect. In fact, don't stand around in the booth playing with your PDA or the Internet.

Don't stand around talking to other staffers. Attendees won't want to walk up to a staffer who is engaged in conversation. Most won't want to interrupt—they'll walk on by.

Don't stand with your back to the aisles. Aisles are where the attendees flow into the booth. Staffers should always be accessible.

Don't sit. Staffers need to look like they are always ready to talk to prospects. If a staffer is sitting, he or she is less approachable. Attendees are more likely to walk on by.

Here are a couple more tips:

Don't put sales literature near the aisles. Place literature inside the exhibit, so that attendees must enter to collect a brochure or pamphlet. Literature placed near an aisle lets attendees scoop and run. In fact, don't be so quick to hand out literature. Remember the whole idea is for your salespeople to *talk* to prospects.

Don't stand at the edge of the booth. Salespeople standing next to the aisle are like guard dogs. They create a barrier between attendees and the exhibit. Standing a few feet inside the booth gives a more open atmosphere. This lets attendees flow in without feeling like they are invading the salesperson's personal space.

Cheat Sheet

The key to getting lots of highly qualified leads is a well-trained booth staff. The savvy booth staffer quickly draws the prospect into the exhibit, qualifies him and moves onto the next prospect. A larger number of highly qualified prospects equal greater potential business for your company down the road.

Generating leads at a trade show is different from other types of sales. The booth staffer has about ten minutes to turn a prospect into a lead—in other words, to make the sale. Therefore, it is imperative that booth staffers have adequate training and preparation; not only on "how to", but also "how not to".

All of the booth staff no-no's covered in this chapter are intuitive, yet we see them perpetrated over and over.

Here is what we learned in this chapter:

- •Untrained booth staffers make mistakes that actually turn prospective leads away.
- •There are three main steps in gathering the wild lead—pulling the prospect in, qualifying him, and letting him go with an agreement to follow up.
- •For more and better leads, train your booth staff. Use in-house programs and consultants. Maintain a library of training materials—books, audio and videotapes.
- •Arm the booth staff with everything they need: a line card with the product's features and benefits, competitive information, a list of the show's events, staff schedule and any other necessary information.
- •Managing the booth staff is a delicate proposition—make sure you've arranged a chain of command, and that all staffers know and understand who is in charge.
- •There are a number of basic rules of conduct, tips and tricks for a more effective event. Make sure your staff know them ahead of time.

Part 3 - Practical Matters: Rolling Up Your Shirt Sleeves and Getting it Done

8

Logistics: The Unglamorous Part of Trade Show Management

The in-laws are coming to Sunday dinner and you're determined to impress them with a fancy meal. Cream of parsley soup, roasted squash with fruited couscous, roasted asparagus with sesame seeds and cherry tomatoes with tomato cream. For dessert you have lemon soufflé.

You planned the meal a week in advance. You checked your food supplies to see what ingredients you already had, and what you needed to get. You reviewed the recipes to be sure you had all the necessary equipment.

Since several of the dishes take more than an hour to prepare and cook, you double check the instructions and plan a strategy. You know just what to do so that everything comes out of the oven and off the stove at the same time. You've already sliced the bell peppers, diced the garlic and crushed the tomatoes.

Like a ballerina, you move through the kitchen preparing each dish. The in-laws are on time, and so is your meal. You planned, checked your supplies, rechecked the recipes and prepared ingredients ahead of time. When it was time to actually cook the meal, you were organized and set to go. The in-laws had a *very* good time.

Trade show logistics are just like cooking a nice meal. It's planning, purchasing, checking and rechecking. Do it well and the company ends up looking like an experienced, professional outfit. Do it poorly and you end up looking like an idiot—a stressed out idiot.

There are three keys to successful trade show logistics: reviewing the exhibitor's manual, ordering and paying for services early, and double-checking your orders one to two weeks before the show. Take these steps and everything within your control will be smooth and flawless.

Within your control. There comes a point when logistical elements of the trade show pass out of your control. The shipment leaves your warehouse, the convention center receives your order and payment, and it's up to the service providers to do their jobs. Most of the time they do. Sometimes they don't. And then there are the occasions when they do their jobs poorly.

We're going to review the exhibitor's manual and show logistics, and also learn a few tips and tricks for preventing service provider foul-ups.

The Exhibitor's Manual Revisited

Show management sends the kit two to three months in advance. Some send their kits as early as four months ahead. Sometimes show management runs into problems, and the kit is late.

The manual, a three-ring binder, is usually mailed to the person whose signature appears on the contract for space rental. If that's not you, be sure the signer makes a note on the contract that the kit and all correspondence should be directed to you.

Some services are time sensitive. Most, like labor, carpet, electrical and telephone services, can wait as late as three weeks prior to the show's opening. But several need to be handled as soon as possible. These include guest passes, exhibitor registration, and company description and product locator for the show guide.

Most large trade shows make sure you receive the pertinent paperwork even if the kit is going to be late. The best way to avoid missed deadlines, though, is to use the online exhibitor's manual.

As soon as you receive the kit, read it through and make a list of all pertinent deadlines. Keep a copy of every service contract and payment you make. Keep copies of the guest pass request, exhibitor registration form, show guide information and every form you provide to show management.

Online Exhibitor's Manuals

Many major shows, such as PC Expo and Comdex, offer exhibitors the ease of online ordering for most show-related services. Show management provides you with the kit's web site address, exhibitor ID and password.

When you order services, you are actually dealing with several different vendors. The paper kit pulls everything together into one binder, with complete instructions on each service.

The exhibitor services portion of the web site is actually a secure portal. From the main page, you can jump to a particular vendor's web site. Vendors provide a page, designed for your specific venue (show), where you can order their service. Always print a paper copy of every contract and form you transmit.

The upside of online ordering is that it is quick, easy and secure. The downsides are these: You cannot use a company check, which many exhibitors prefer to do. Rather, online ordering requires a company credit card to pay for the services. Also, the online exhibitor's manual is not always up and running before the paper kit arrives.

Whether you use the paper kit or the online version, always confirm that the vendor has received your order and payment.

Complimentary Guest Passes and Exhibitor Registration

All trade shows charge an entrance fee. It can cost an attendee $65 or more to gain access to the exhibits. But many attendees get in without paying a dime because one or more exhibitors give them complimentary guest passes.

Trade show management provides exhibitors with an endless supply of passes, and the best part is—they don't cost you, the exhibitor, a dime. If you request more than a certain amount, usually 2,500, most shows pre-print the exhibitor's company name and booth number on the guest passes, at no charge. Unfortunately, the free guest pass is for admittance to the exhibits only. Everything else, lectures, seminars and meetings are extra.

Order your guest passes as soon as you receive the exhibitor's manual. Be sure to indicate whether you want your company name and booth number printed on the passes.

Fulfillment of guest pass orders slows down as show time approaches because many exhibitors wait to put in their request. So, instead of taking two weeks, it may take four or six weeks for the passes to arrive. Trade show management usually hires another company to print and fulfill the orders. Once you place the order, it is out of their control.

Give yourself enough time ordering guest passes, to avoid the last minute rush. You'll want those passes ready to go out with your pre-show mailings. Your guests should receive the passes with enough time to pre-register. They must fill out the guest pass form: name, address, company, position and so forth, and mail it several weeks in advance. They receive an attendee name badge a week or two before the show. Otherwise, your guest must pick up their badge at the show, usually standing in a long line.

An alternative to paper passes is on-line registration for complimentary guest admission. Instead of mailing paper passes, you provide your guests with a key code and web address. Using the code, your guest accesses the registration web site on the Internet and pre-register themselves. On-line registration saves time and money. On the other hand, it doesn't have the visual impact of a paper guest pass and your sales letter.

Exhibitor registration lets you pre-register all of your booth personnel. Submit the form at least three or four weeks before the show so that management can send the prepared name badges.

Anyone registering later must wait to pick up his or her badge at the show. Standing in long lines at the Exhibitor Registration Desk is a frustrating way to start the workday.

The exhibitor name badge is your pass to enter the exhibit hall. Without it, security guards posted at the entrance will not let you in. As registered exhibitors, you and your booth personnel have access to the show floor as soon as set-up begins.

Filling out the exhibitor registration form is a simple procedure but it can be time consuming. Here's what you can do to keep it from being an all-day job. Compile your list of booth personnel ahead of time and make sure each name is spelled correctly. You also need each person's job title, telephone number and extension, facsimile number, e-mail and mailing address.

Make a photo copy or two of the blank form and file the extras. The form provides space to register several people. Fill in the preliminary information at the top of a blank form: Company name, booth number, address, telephone number, web address, your name and job title. If you are bringing in personnel from satellite offices, fill out separate forms with the office's contact information.

Make photocopies of the partially completed forms. This way, if you need more than one form, you avoid wasting time filling out the same contact information. On one of the copies, begin filling in the registration information for your booth personnel.

Fax the completed forms to the number provided. File the forms with your other completed contracts and save the extra photocopies. You can register more personnel right up to the week before the show—a day or two before set-up begins.

As with the guest passes, you can register your personnel on-line. Just access the on-line exhibitor's manual and you are directed to the exhibitor registration page. The electronic procedure is identical to the paper method. Make sure you print a copy of each session for your files.

Telephone and Electrical Services

The good news is the contracts and payments are not due until two or three weeks before the show. The bad news is there are no

"Early Bird Specials" for sending payment before the deadline. More bad news, there is no on-line ordering option. So, pull out your ball-point pen. Most forms have four copies, so be sure to write firmly.

The local phone company provides telecommunication service. However, the convention center staff handles the contracts, labor and payment.

There are several benefits to having a telephone in your booth. The most important one is that you can stay in constant contact with the home office. Salespeople won't miss messages from important clients and they won't have to stand in line at the pay phones to check in. You can e-mail the leads to the home office each evening.

On the other hand, the service is relatively expensive. One phone line can cost up to $250. Out-going long distance calls are extra. You can bypass the extra cost of renting a phone line by taking the company's cell phone, however using the cell phone can be almost as expensive. What's more, the noisy convention floor and the building's metal roof make for exceptionally poor sound quality.

In addition to the telephone line, the telecommunication services offer extra voice lines, a facsimile line and ISDN service.

Remember that not all convention centers include a handset (telephone) with the service. Read the contract form carefully. You may need to order equipment separately. The telecommunications service provider needs to know where you want the telephone, ISDN line and facsimile in your booth. Use the simple map provided on the form to indicate to installers where to place the line or lines.

Some convention centers assign telephone numbers a few days or a week before the start of the show. The service provider can often give you the number when you call to verify receipt of your order and payment.

After the show, expect an additional bill from the telecommunications service provider for long distance charges. You or your Accounts Receivable Manager should receive it about a month after the show ends. Be sure to make a copy for your records.

The convention center also handles electrical services. The electrical service provider needs three pieces of information from you:

•How many outlets do you need?

•What wattage do you need in each outlet?

•Where do you want the outlets placed?

How many outlets do you need? Does your exhibit have lights? You need one outlet for every set of lights. Do your product demonstrations require power? Are you using audio/visual equipment for your presentation? Are you putting a cappuccino machine in the booth?

What wattage do you need in each outlet? Most exhibit equipment—lights, audio/visual and so forth, have minimum requirements. Some equipment such as an industrial-style popcorn maker may require more. Your product demonstration may involve several pieces of power draining equipment. Check the technical specifications on your lights, audiovisual and product demonstrations.

Resist the temptation to cut corners. Be safe. Order enough outlets and enough power for each piece of equipment.

Where do you want the outlets placed? Electrical labor (yes, that's what they are called), need to know where you want each outlet installed. The order form provides a simple grid box you can use to specify the location for each outlet, or "drop".

Both the telecommunications and electrical service forms and payment are due two to three weeks before the show opens. You need to provide credit card information on both forms, or send a separate check for each service. Even though you may send payment to the same address and make checks out to the same business entity, each service requires separate payment.

Lights Out Request

The "lights out request" is simply a form to tell show management that you want them to turn out any convention center lights above your booth space. You only need to do this if convention center lighting interferes with your own exhibit's lights or staged presentations. There is no payment involved, although you do have a deadline.

Labor

If your exhibit is a portable pop-up, you can set it up in less than 15 minutes, you don't need to hire labor, right? What about the company sign that mounts on top of the back wall? You need a ladder to install that, so you need labor.

Convention centers have rules about who gets to set-up and tear-down your exhibit. The rules may vary from venue to venue, but generally, they go like this:

To set the exhibit up yourself, two people should be able to set it up in less than 15 minutes. One person can take as long as half an hour. You have to be able to erect the entire exhibit without the use of a ladder.

If the exhibit needs more than two people to set up, takes longer than the threshold 15 or 30 minutes, or you need a ladder, you must hire labor. You need union labor.

The convention center provides union labor. The order form included in the exhibitor's manual lets you reserve two or more laborers. You estimate how many you need to set up the exhibit, how many hours it takes to set up and when you want to set up. Fill out the form and calculate the cost. Be sure to write in the date and time you plan to be at the labor desk to pick up your team.

There are a few danger areas to keep your eye on when making arrangements. The first is timing. If you set-up and tear-down during normal business hours— nine a.m. to five p.m., you are charged "straight time", usually in the $52 to $54 dollar an hour range, per person. If you set-up and tear-down after 5 p.m. or on the weekend, you pay time and a half, which works out to $77 to $81 and hour. If you have the bad luck to set-up or tear-down on a holiday, you end up paying double-time.

Plan to set your exhibit up after electrical and telephone service and carpeting are installed. Be prepared for problems in your plan. You may schedule labor for a certain date and time, only to find the carpet hasn't been installed. This is a common occurrence—the **Set-**

up and Tear-down section later in this chapter shows you how to handle this and many other show-site snafus.

Plan to supervise the entire process. Arrive at your booth well in advance of your planned set-up time. You'll need the extra time to solve problems and track down missing shipments. Pick up your laborers at the labor desk on time. If you need to delay set-up for any reason—perhaps you need to wait until the carpet is installed—let the supervisor know before the scheduled pick up time.

Don't try to skirt the convention center's labor rules. If you try to set up your complicated exhibit yourself, the convention center usually finds out. By breaking the rules, you face significant fines. You also end up paying the full cost for labor to set up your exhibit. Besides, labor is well-trained and more efficient at setting up and tearing down exhibits than are your own staff.

Exhibitor Appointed Contractor (EAC)

An alternative to convention center labor is to hire an outside company. Of course, the outside contractor must also be a member of the labor union. Outside contractors are more expensive, about $4 or more an hour. Most have a four-hour minimum; that is, you must hire them for at least four hours.

An outside contractor competes with the convention center and with other EACs for business. He specializes in trade show set-up and tear-down and often works closely with exhibit manufacturers. Most importantly, he is available for tasks convention center labor is not. He will run to the airport to pick up that crate that didn't ship with the rest of the exhibit.

The contractor depends on repeat business and referrals from satisfied customers. He or she wants to do a good job for you. They are experienced trade show experts and probably know more about setting up your exhibit than you do. Ask your exhibit manufacturer for referrals. Ask other exhibitors whom they use.

You must let trade show management know that you plan to use an outside contractor about a month or so before the show. Fill out the form, giving the name, address and phone number of your contractor. Fax or mail the form to the appropriate address, and keep a copy for your files.

Hanging Signs

A great way to draw attention to your exhibit is to hang a sign from the ceiling above it. Your logo or company name is visible throughout the convention center hall.

Your sign is part of your exhibit. You store it with your other property, care for and refurbish it just as you do your exhibit. But when it comes to shipping and setting it up, the hanging sign is handled separately.

The labor order form for having the sign installed above your booth is separate from other labor forms. The work is specialized, and you pay a higher hourly rate. Send the form to the appropriate address with payment about six to eight weeks before the show.

Ship the sign, along with detailed instructions on how to put it together, a week or two before the rest of your exhibit. The order form gives you the deadline for having your sign at the convention center.

Furniture

This category includes simple tables and chairs, table drapes, office furniture, waste paper baskets and basic custom carpets and carpet padding. It also includes premium furniture, custom carpet and padding, even exhibit rentals.

If you own your own exhibit, you probably don't need to rent furniture. If you also own your own carpet, you may get to skip this set of forms altogether.

However, furniture rental is a great way to enhance an existing exhibit. Small exhibitors can put together a good-looking exhibit through rentals alone. Decorating companies catering to trade shows offer a variety of furniture, exhibit pieces and carpet. At least one company lets you view samples and order on-line.

Furniture order forms are separate from carpet forms, though payment is made in one lump, to the decorating company. Check the forms for "early-bird special" deadlines. Ordering in advance can save you up 10% on rental costs.

Drayage

This is an old-fashioned term for material handling. Within the context of trade shows, it simply refers to the act of moving your exhibit shipment from the convention center's loading dock to your booth, and back again after the show. You must estimate the weight of your total exhibit shipment, calculate the cost of drayage and prepay for labor.

The cost is per 100 pounds. For example, if drayage is charged at $50 per 100 pounds and your shipment weighs 2,000 pounds, you pay a total of $2,000. That's $1,000 coming in, and $1,000 going out.

The good news is that if you overestimate on your calculations, show management reimburses the difference. The bad new is, some convention centers charge extra for very small shipments. This is a particular problem for exhibitors who split their shipments. More bad news, there is no "early bird special" for sending payment in advance.

Plant Rental

Sometimes an exhibit needs a little something extra. A small plant here, a floral arrangement there can liven up drab booths. Plants can also hide imperfections in your booth such as damaged panels and unattractive seams.

Renting plants is more expensive than buying similar arrangements. However, the convenience is usually worth it. You don't have to haul the plants in and out of the convention center. And you don't have to figure out what to do with the plant after the show is over.

Booth Cleaning

Trade shows are a messy business. Set-up is messy—bits of packing tape, waded up paper, trash all over the place. The booth cleaning service dusts and cleans and vacuums in preparation for the show's opening. They will even shampoo your carpet.

For six or eight hours a day, people walk through your exhibit, dropping bits of trash, filling up the wastebaskets. The cleaning service will vacuum and empty trash each evening.

For basic services, simply calculate your booth's area and multiply by the going rate. Multiply that result by the number of days the trade show takes place and you have the cost of keeping your booth clean.

Say your booth space is 400 square feet. The booth cleaning service charges $.20 per square foot to clean the booth in preparation for opening day. They charge $.15 per square foot on the remaining days. The show opens on Tuesday and closes on Thursday. Here's what you pay:

Show opening: 400 sq. ft. x $.20 per sq. ft. x 1 = $40

During show: 400 sq. ft. x $.15 per sq. ft. x 2 = $120

Grand total: $160

Order Recap and Credit Card Information

The recap form is a place where you can record all of your installation and decoration (I&D) orders and expenses. These include labor, drayage, hanging sign installation, plant rental, carpet and furniture.

The advantage is that you can add up all the charges and write one check or make one credit card payment for the services. Even though the services come from different companies, you make only one payment to trade show management. They divide the payments and forward the forms.

The recap form serves another purpose. You must provide trade show management with your company's credit card information. Here's how it works: on the last day of the trade show, management recalculates all of your I&D services. You may have used more labor than you'd anticipated, or maybe you unexpectedly needed the booth cleaning services to shampoo your carpet. All of these items must be paid for by the end of the trade show. Management bills the difference to the credit card you provide on the Order Recap form.

You must provide valid credit card information, even if you are paying by company check. If you do not, show management will not process your orders.

Not included are telecommunications and electrical service and lead retrieval rental. These are not considered installation and decoration items. Also, not all trade shows use the Order Recap and Credit Card Information form; though most do. However, all shows require all accounts to be settled by the end of the event.

Shipping

Shipping is a necessary evil. Unless the trade show is within driving distance, and your exhibit equipment is small enough to fit in the trunk of your car, you'll need to ship it via truck or van line.

Choosing a company to transport your exhibit is an important decision. You want someone who will get the job done and handle your equipment with care. On the other hand, you want to keep your expenses down.

When it comes to selecting a company to transport your equipment, you have two basic choices. You can hire a small trucking company that charges less. Or you can hire a van line or trucking company that specializes in trade show transportation, and which charges more—sometimes a lot more.

Spend more money and get a higher quality transportation company. Or spend less and get a lower quality company and save your budget at the same time. But do you really save money with the cheaper trucking company? Here's how the two types of transportation companies differ. Read up, and then decide.

An inexpensive trucking company is a small, independent operation, sometimes local. The drivers are not union members. The company charges you based on the weight and dimension of your shipment. You schedule them to pick up your trade show equipment from your storage facility at the appointed time and date. The truck arrives, the driver copies your invoice to his "bill of lading", a billing and inventory form. Your people load the equipment onto the truck. The driver hands you a copy of his bill of lading and drives away.

A short time later, the truck pulls up to its main facility, your equipment is unloaded and reloaded onto the vehicle that will carry it to the convention center. The new truck may belong to your trucking company, or it may be another trucking company, one with whom your trucker has a cooperative agreement.

You see, the trucking company you hired may not be able to send a vehicle to the far away convention center at this time. Or he may be able to cut his costs by forming a loose cooperative with other independent companies. One handles one part of the country and another handles another area.

The truck carrying your equipment arrives at the convention center during your targeted move-in day. Trade show management tells you when they want your equipment to arrive at the convention center loading dock. Let's say your targeted move-in is Friday between noon and five p.m. Your truck pulls up at one o'clock and waits to be unloaded...along with dozens of other trucks.

So your truck waits and waits. The driver is not a member of a union. The convention center's loading dock workers are. They will always give preferential treatment to other union members. Your trucking company charges you for the time its drivers sit and wait to be unloaded.

The return shipment at the end of the trade show is exactly the reverse of getting your equipment to the show.

On the other hand, van lines charge more to get your equipment to the trade show, but they have divisions that specialize in transporting trade show equipment. You pay more, but you get additional service. Here's the scenario with a van line or trucking company specializing in trade show transportation:

You've made arrangements with the van line a month or more before the trade show. A week and a half to two weeks before the show, a truck shows up at your storage facility, at the appointed time, to pick up your equipment. Your people load the equipment onto the truck. The truck driver counts the pieces and fills out a detailed bill of lading. You get a copy of his paper work and he gets a copy of yours.

The truck pulls away from your facility. The driver may drive to his company's central facility where your equipment is re-loaded onto another truck. Or he may continue on to the convention center.

Because the van line or trucking company specializes in trade show transport, they likely have other customers exhibiting at the same show. Your equipment is probably keeping company with other exhibitor's equipment.

If you have material that requires special handling, something perishable, or delicate instruments, the van line or trucking company can handle it.

So, the truck travels to the convention center; your equipment enjoys a quieter, less bumpy ride. The truck arrives in the destination city, perhaps a day before your targeted move in date and time. The transportation company has a central location near or at the convention center where they can wait for a day or so. At the appropriate time, the truck rolls up to the convention center loading dock. Convention center labor unloads the truck, the truck and driver move on to their next assignment.

The truck carrying your equipment didn't have to wait in line very long at the loading dock. The driver and convention center workers belong to the same labor union, so they have a special rapport.

You don't have to pay the trucking company extra because the driver had to wait in line. Your equipment has less wear and tear because the higher quality truck or van offers a smoother ride.

As a special bonus, van lines and trucking companies specializing in trade show transportation let you track the progress of your shipment. At any given moment as your equipment makes its way across the country, you can call up and find out exactly where it is.

In the short term, inexpensive trucking companies who do not specialize in trade show transportation and who are not members of a labor union, are less expensive. You may need to work a little harder, worry a bit more, but you save money.

In the long term, the expenses of using a low budget trucking company add up. The trucks give a rougher ride. Your exhibit's shipping containers accumulate more damage and wear. Containers account for as much as one third of the cost of your exhibit. If you expect them to last five years, but they last only three, your budget suffers. The rough ride can even damage your exhibit.

Whichever you choose, a company that specializes in trade show transportation or low cost trucking company, there are a few things you need to remember as you plan your shipment.

Contact your transportation company a few months before the show. Let them know when and where you are exhibiting, and that you will need service to and from the convention center. Make arrangements with the company to pick up and deliver your equipment to the convention center on or after your targeted move-in date. Also, make arrangements for your transportation company to pick up your equipment from the convention center after the show, at a particular date and time.

Remember that some convention centers levy a fine if your shipment arrives before your targeted move-in.

Inform trade show management that your trucking company will pick up your equipment after the show ends. During the trade show, management gives you a few forms to fill out and return before the end of the show.

One of these is a form that lets you tell management which trucking company you are using for your return shipment. Be sure to fill it out completely and return it to the appropriate service desk. Otherwise, management will hand your equipment over to the show's official freight company—usually more expensive than your trucker or van line.

Set-Up and Tear-Down

Set-up is the last item on your list of things to do before the show opens. It is one of the most critical events in trade show planning. Unfortunately, things can and do go wrong. But there are several things you can do to avoid last-minute meltdowns.

First on the list, arrange and pay for all of your services well before the show. Do not wait until you arrive at the convention center to contract for electricity, telephone, carpet, furniture or any service or materials that you can order ahead of time.

No matter how simple your exhibit, waiting until the last minute to make arrangements can be disastrous. You pay higher prices. Worse, you end up with worn or defective equipment, threadbare carpet and dilapidated furniture. The lead retrieval service may run out of units, leaving you without an easy way to capture leads.

Next, set up your exhibit *at least* one day before the show opens. In fact, for all but the simplest exhibits, set up as soon as the space and services become available.

Suppose your exhibit is so small that you can hand carry the entire load into the convention center, and set up in less than half an hour? The show opens at ten am. Can you show up at seven and still set up in time for the show's opening? Often, yes. But not always.

If you wait until the last minute to set up, you leave no time to take care of last-minute problems. And at some point in everyone's trade show career, something goes wrong. Electrical service loses your request form and your booth has no electrical power. The decoration people put in the wrong color carpet. Lots of things can go wrong. You need to give yourself enough time to resolve whatever problems arise.

If your exhibit takes two hours to set up, give yourself at least four. If it takes four hours to set up, budget a full day. If it takes eight hours, give yourself a full day and a half minimum, to set everything up, trouble shoot product demonstrations and resolve any service-related problems.

Include in your budget the cost of arriving before your scheduled set-up. Verify that the electrical and telephone services are installed, and supervise the installation of your exhibit's carpet. This way, you are assured that the carpet is installed *on top of* the electrical cords and that outlets emerge from the carpet in exactly the right places.

As soon as you first arrive at your booth site, follow this simple checklist:

•Verify that your telephone service in installed

•If you are supplying your own handset, hook it up and make sure it is working.

•Verify that your electrical service is installed and functioning properly.

If you've specified that the lead retrieval unit is to be delivered to your booth, check to see that it has arrived safely and intact. If you are to pick it up from the lead retrieval service desk, wait until after you've inventoried your equipment, or send a colleague to pick up the unit.

Inventory your equipment. The entire shipment, theoretically, is already delivered and sitting in your booth space. If anything at all is missing, your first stop should be the drayage or material handling service desk.

Next on your list of set-up things to do is to have the carpet installed. If you brought your own, you will be using convention center labor or an exhibitor appointed contractor.

Do not install the carpet yourself. Even if you and your colleagues can install it in 15 minutes, hire labor to do it. If you install carpet yourself, you may save money in the short term. But if during the show someone trips on a badly installed carpet and injures him or herself, your company is legally liable. Better that the injured party sues the convention center.

Once the carpet is in, the real set-up begins: erecting the booth and displays.

Tear-down is a lot less violent than it sounds. It is also one of the most important steps in preparing for your next trade show. Tear-down officially begins the moment the trade show ends on the last day. By the time the last day rolls around, everyone is exhausted. Often, foot traffic has died down as attendees head home. It is tempting to start packing up early.

Some of your staff will be in a hurry to go home. It may be tempting to rush through tear-down. Don't do it. Be patient and take your time. The more care you take during tear-down, the better off you will be setting up your next trade show.

If you have a simple exhibit that you can tear down without labor, wait until after the show ends. If show management stored your shipping containers, you will need to wait until the containers are delivered to your booth. Don't leave demonstration equipment unattended during tear-down.

If your exhibit is more elaborate, here's what you can do to make sure tear-down goes smoothly:

- Make sure you've informed show management who your transportation company will be, and approximately when they will pick up your shipment. Show management provides a form for you to write down all the pertinent information. The form appears in your booth, along with the final bill, before the floor opens on the last day. Fill out the form, and *return it* to the appropriate service desk.
- As soon as the show closes, pack up the lead retrieval unit. Assign a colleague to return the unit to the service desk as soon as possible. Make sure your colleague gives you the return receipt, which you will keep in your files.

Inventory your exhibit as you prepare it for shipment. Use your original inventory list.

Repack each piece of the exhibit in its original crate or box. If parts one through ten arrived in crate A, return them in crate A.

Make sure each crate and box is packed carefully. If a piece of equipment or booth needs to be individually wrapped to keep it safe from damage during the return shipment, take the time to do it properly.

"Tear-down" and "move out" can be a lot of "hurry up and wait." Waiting for your crates and boxes to be delivered back to your booth. Waiting for labor. Remember to relax, take your time and do it properly.

All About On-Site Show Services

As we learned earlier, different vendors handle different services. The convention center manages labor and drayage. They may also coordinate electrical and telecommunications services. Furniture and carpet are handled through an independent decorator.

You may order your lead retrieval from Frank in Atlanta. You talk to your trade show management sales representative in her office in New York. But a week before the trade show opens, all of your contacts relocate to the convention center.

Decorating, lead retrieval, trade show management, booth cleaning; all of the representatives pack up on Friday afternoon a week or so before the show, and head to the show site. The following Monday, at the convention center, they set up their service desks, hook up their phones and start work at their new bases of operations.

Now, if you need to talk to your sales representatives, you must contact them at their temporary offices, at the show site. If you are not at the convention center yourself, ordering or changing service requests is cumbersome and difficult. Your representatives may leave the office early that Friday before traveling. They may arrive late Monday. In other words, they may be incommunicado for a few working days. And they may be hard pressed to help you long-distance.

Here's what you need to know about on-site show services:

Most trade show services maintain service desks at the convention center. Company representatives are available and ready to help you a full week before the show opens.

It's easier to work with the service desk personnel in person. The week before the trade show is busy. On-site personnel are focusing on exhibitors already at the convention center, helping them set up.

Although it's not a good idea, it is possible to order or change many services at the show site. It's also possible that you will lose out on a service if you wait until the last minute. The electricians may not be able to provide power to your booth. The telecommunications company may not be able to provide a phone line. You may want to rent a blue carpet and find all that remains is a dilapidated orange thing.

Overnight couriers such as UPS or Federal Express maintain a presence at larger convention centers. The courier company provides a full service desk, allowing you to send and receive overnight packages before and during the show. The service delivers packages right to your booth. However, they don't deliver during show hours.

Many trade shows provide exhibitors with their own lounge area, often with light refreshments. You should make it a priority to locate the lounge at the earliest opportunity.

There are a few other people working the service desks in addition to your representative. These will be the folks handing you your lead retrieval unit, your exhibitor badge holder, helping you settle your end-of-show accounts. Trade shows are inherently stress-filled events-on both sides of the desk. Service desk personnel spend up to two weeks at the receiving end of a lot of frustrated, tired exhibitors, salespeople, marketing managers, trade show coordinators and corporate VIPs. Be nice to them. They deserve it.

Cheat Sheet

Trade show logistics are unsexy and unglamorous and the only time they are exciting is when things go *wrong*. On the other hand, they are the backbone of any trade show effort. Logistics is the shopping list for the gourmet meal, the step-by-step process of managing the trade show.

The bulk of the shopping list is contained in the exhibitor's manual, a notebook filled with forms and information on trade show services and marketing opportunities. Whereas booth staff training and advertising and public relations provide the sizzle of trade show management, logistics provides the structure. The backbone. Without it, your trade show effort would collapse.

Here's what we covered in this chapter:

- The exhibitor's manual contains most of the forms and contact information you'll need to coordinate your event.
- When hiring a shipping company to transport your exhibit equipment to and from the convention center, consider not only cost, but quality and convenience.
- Set-up and tear-down are breeding grounds for trade show tragedy—give them your complete attention and care.
- Show services sets up help desks at the convention center several days before the show opens.

9

Tips and Tricks for the Happy Trade Show Manager

Managing trade shows is a delicate operation. We've talked about all of the elements that go into producing a great event: planning, organizing, exhibit design, graphics, advertising and public relations, booth staff training and logistics. We've covered some of the nuances of trade show management, such as interdepartmental cooperation, managing the program when you are not in charge, everything you need to know in order to exhibit. But….

The sad truth is, things go wrong. Despite all of your careful planning, problems crop up. As any experienced trade show manager will tell you, you can count on at least one thing to go wrong during each trade show. It can be as small as forgetting to pack your dress shoes, or as big as losing your entire exhibit during shipment.

Now, both of these problems have obvious solutions—go out and buy a pair of dress shoes before the show opens (affordable) and go out and rent an exhibit or table and chairs at the last minute (very expensive).

The good news is, when things go wrong during the planning and coordinating phases, you have the resources and time to make corrections. The bad news is, when things go wrong at the show, time and help are what you *don't* have.

This chapter is devoted to helping you get through those emergencies, large and small. There are three things you can do to help yourself.

First, after each show save all of the paperwork, notes, names telephone and fax numbers, e-mail addresses, forms, contracts, maps, everything related to the event. You or your successor can refer to the file or notebook you've created, planning for next year's exhibition.

Be sure to include a copy of your post-show report. Also include notes about things such as unusual convention center construction—the over-hanging balcony that lowers the ceiling height above part of the floor plan, and booth 1104's theft problem. You may notice a pattern over time, such as a consistent theft problem at a particular facility (it happens.)

Pick a counterpart back at the office. Choose someone who is familiar with what you do for a living and who has access to your office, files and computer. Your office backup should be available to you 24-hours a day, have access to the Internet and be willing to do whatever is necessary to help out in an emergency.

Second, make sure that your backup person has an exact duplicate of your master file with copies of all contracts, forms, names, contact information, maps, schedules, everything you have in your file or notebook. This includes the name, street address and telephone number of your hotel, rental car information, airline reservation information and company credit card number. It also includes your company's Fed Ex or UPS account number and a supply of letter packs, name and home phone number of each booth staff member, everything he or she might need at a moment's notice.

And last, start and maintain your own Trade Show bible. Create a section for the names and contact information of everyone that has ever helped or provided a trade show-related service. Include hotels, airports, airport limousine services, airlines and car rental services you've used. And don't forget to add in the addresses of office supply stores, mini-malls and hardware stores located near the convention center or hotel. Organize your bible in a fashion that suits you. Add sections, as you become a proficient trade show manager.

Here is your bible's most important section: *Troubleshooting*. Every time you encounter and resolve a problem, write it down. Include all the details; who, what, when, where, why, how much. Listen to the horror stories other exhibitor's tell, and write those down as well. A number of problems and their solutions are outlined below. Go ahead and use them to start your bible's troubleshooting section.

Problems and Solutions

🖉 **Problem**: The shipment arrived at the convention center, missing a box or crate. The item never shows up and you are forced to replace it. How do you track down who is responsible for the lost item, and hold them accountable?

🖉 **Solution**: Unfortunately, in most cases you will be unable to determine who lost the item. You can file a claim with your trucker. But unless you can prove, through paperwork, that the item was lost in transit, your claim will go nowhere.

Here is the most likely sequence of events leading up to the loss:

Ready to ship, you write up an inventory of boxes and crates. You and your shipping clerk prepare the shipment. You trucker copies your inventory onto his bill of lading, gives you a copy and drives off.

1. Possibility number one, somewhere along the way, your trucker reorganizes his load, perhaps picking up or delivering another shipment, separating one of your items from the rest. At the convention center, the trucker delivers your shipment, minus the lost box or crate. The loading dock labor copies the trucker's bill of lading onto his own form without checking the shipment and accepts the full load. The paperwork says the entire shipment was delivered, but you're still down one item.

2. Possibility number two, your trucker arrives at the convention center with your shipment intact. Labor unloads your exhibit, copies the trucker's bill of lading (without checking the shipment.) Somewhere between the loading dock and your booth, labor loses one of your boxes or crates. Neither trade show management, labor, nor any other service contractors can be held liable for the loss of the item. It says so in the contract you signed a year ago, renting the exhibit space. Re-read the section titled, "Liability and Insurance".

So, how do you minimize your losses? First of all, make sure your own facilities' insurance covers the loss of items shipped to a convention. If it does not, contract for special, temporary insurance, designed for special events.

Second, consolidate your shipment as much as possible. Pack all boxes onto wooden pallets, strap them down, place "DO NOT DE-PALLETIZE" signs in all the obvious places and cover the entire pallet with shrink-wrap. This step alone will prevent most losses.

✏ **Problem**: You've had expensive equipment stolen right out of your booth. Perhaps one of your computers or monitors disappeared after the show. You returned the next morning only to find boxes missing.

Or, during the show somewhere, somehow, someone managed to steal the memory from the little hand-held military computer on display in your exhibit.

How do you minimize the risk of theft in an admittedly vulnerable situation?

✏ **Solution**: There are several things you can do to avoid losses due to theft.

- •Don't pack expensive products in their original cartons. That 30-inch flatbed LCD computer monitor just begs to be stolen. And during the chaos of set-up or tear-down, it's an easy job.
- •Stay with your exhibit after the show until all boxes are properly packed, palletized and strapped in place. Trade show thieves are more apt to grab and run. Packing up and palletizing make it too inconvenient for the theft-minded.

- Hire security. A security guard can watch over your equipment while the show is not in session. There are a couple of drawbacks to hired guns. It's an expensive service, and there is also no guarantee that the extra security will prevent theft.
- Make sure that all of your expensive equipment is secure. Laptop computers and other small items should locked to the display stand. Components, even when the main feature is easy removability, should be secure from light fingers.
- If you want to display the internal design of your fancy new widget, put a piece of clear Plexiglas in place of the side panel. Hardware stores carry a nifty little item called the security screw and security screwdriver. Use security screws instead of the chassis's normal hardware to lock the Plexiglas into place.
- Finally, if the display equipment is for looks only and you won't be demonstrating the product, leave expensive components at home. If it won't be visible to attendees, there's no need to bring along all that expensive memory.

✎ **Problem**: You lost all of the leads collected from the last trade show. How do you prevent this in the future—and save your job?

✎ **Solution**: Believe it or not, this happens a lot. And not just to inexperienced exhibitors. First of all, do not toss your paper leads into the exhibit crate, expecting to retrieve them back at the home office. So many things can go wrong with this method of transport.

Fed Ex or UPS your leads back to the home office at the end of the show. If it's in your budget, send them back every night. The best solution, though, is to rent a lead retrieval unit that produces both paper leads and an electronic file. At the end of the show you have paper and a diskette.

E-mail the electronic file back to the home office each evening.

✎ **Problem**: In preparing the shipment, you neglect to send the entire exhibit. Worse, you don't catch your mistake until set-up day. How do you deal with the problem of a partial booth? How do you prevent such a mistake from happening again?

✎ **Solution**: Amazingly, this is not an unfamiliar story. Part of the exhibit is misdirected during shipment, or the exhibitor omits an integral component. If this happens to you, there are two possible courses you can take.

First, if the exhibit component is still in your warehouse, you may be able to have the item sent via airfreight to the convention center, overnight. With a lot of money, and a bit of luck, you can be up and running before the show opens. This is an "iffy" proposition due to several limitations. You may be limited by the physical size of the crate. Larger crates must ship in wide body aircraft. These aircraft fly less often than you would expect. Also, not all airports accommodate them.

You may be limited by time, as well. If you cannot transport your crate to an airport air cargo facility in time, you've lost the race before leaving the starting block. Measure your crate, call your van line if you are using someone who specializes in trade show transport, or the airfreight company at the nearest international airport and book passage for your equipment. You must also arrange transportation for the crate from the airport to the convention center.

The other solution is to simply rent furniture to replace the missing exhibit. Many exhibitors who go this route report success, often taking in more leads than they expected.

Of course, the best solution is to make sure your entire exhibit arrives intact, on time. If your transportation company fails to deliver, hire a different outfit next time.

If the problem is on *your* end, here are some tips to help you along.

Personally supervise everything. Supervise the transfer of your exhibit from the warehouse to the shipping area. Supervise the loading of the equipment onto the truck or van.

Prepare an inventory list ahead of time. Start your list with the exhibit crates. For example, you have three crates containing your exhibit. Label them Crate 1, 2, and 3.

Inventory your shipment when it is completely queued for shipment. Label each box, list the box and its contents on your inventory sheet. If you are putting boxes on pallets, indicate on your inventory list which boxes are going on which pallets.

Arrange to send your shipment on a day when your shipping department is not busy. For most companies, Fridays is a very busy day. Check with the department, and ship on an earlier day.

✍ **Problem**: You find that you spend too much for electrical services; or you want to cut your show services budget. How do you save on your budget without cutting corners?

✍ **Solution**: You can minimize the amount of money you spend on electrical services by making sure your entire exhibit is "plug-and-play". Avoid equipment that requires hard wiring, where the electrician actually has to connect wire to wire. This takes far longer to install.

Also, run your under-the-carpet electrical before your freight is delivered to the booth. That way your electrician won't have to wait around while you move the crates out of the booth so that he can work.

One last tip, pack extra power strips and heavy duty extension cords with your set-up supplies. You won't waste time or money when you have to halt set-up and run out to the local supply store to buy supplies.

✍ **Problem**: You arrive at the convention center, unpack your equipment and find that your graphics appear scratched. What can you do to repair or minimize the appearance of the damage?

✍ **Solution**: Start by cleaning the graphics surface. But first, check to be sure that the laminate surface is water-resistant. Check the seal on the edges. Also be sure that the scratch doesn't go all the way through to the graphic.

If the scratch is actually bits of glue or smears, you can clean them up with a bit of alcohol and a scratch-resistant cloth. You can also use simple soap and water. But never use anything that contains ammonia, which may damage the surface.

If you have a genuine scratch, which does not penetrate to the graphic, a coat of clear nail polish may conceal the damage.

If the graphic is lit from behind, you can try moving the light to a different position, shifting the focus from the scratched area.

Problem: You arrive at the convention center, unpack your equipment, and notice a chip in a laminate tabletop. What can you do to hide or minimize the damage?

Solution: You can minimize the appearance of some chips by filling them in with colored caulk. Include in your set-up kit colored caulk that closely matches all of the laminate in your exhibit.

You can hide deep scratches with the stroke of a colored grease pencil. So, also include in your kit a supply of wood repair pencils, available in any hardware store.

Problem: You arrive at the convention center, unfurl your carpet, which you own, and notice a big ugly hole. What can you do to affect a temporary repair? How can you hide or minimize the appearance of the damage?

Solution: First, try duct tape, the universal cure-all. For small tears, start by cutting away the frayed edges and tape the edges together on the carpet's backside. After the carpet is installed, comb the seam to hide the fix.

If the tear is rather large and obvious, you might try using a piece of carpet from a hidden area of the exhibit. Use a straight knife to cut away and clean up the edges of the tear. Measure the damaged area and cut away an appropriate-sized section of carpet from a hidden part of the exhibit, such as under a display stand. Use duct tape to tape the piece in place.

The method most experienced exhibitors prefer for large tears, is the camouflage technique. Rent a plant or move a piece of exhibit to cover the damage. Have the carpet repaired or replaced after returning from the show.

Use these problems and their solutions to start your own Trade Show bible Troubleshooting section. As you coordinate more events you will experience more problems; add those to your list. Keep your eyes and ears open, watch how other exhibitors solve *their* problems.

Talk to others, ask them about their trade show snafus. People who manage and coordinate their company's events love to recount horror stories and compare war wounds.

Can you guess why this document is called a Trade Show *bible*? Because it is filled with all the information you need to coordinate events and handle the inevitable last minute tangles. So take good care of yours! And always keep a back-up copy in a safe place.

Cheat Sheet

No matter how hard you work and how carefully you plan, something usually goes wrong. It may be a minor problem, or a major disaster. Often it is something you've never encountered before.

Start now to organize a notebook of information—a bible filled with all the general information you need to organize trade shows. Contact names and numbers, service providers and more. Include solutions to every problem you can think of. Collect stories from other managers and put them in as well.

Most importantly, when something goes wrong, stay calm. No matter what the problem, you'll solve it more efficiently if you do not panic.

Here are some of the problems we covered in this chapter:

- Theft can be a problem, so take precautions to avoid losing equipment to light fingers.
- Part of your exhibit can be lost during transport from your storage facility to your trade show booth space, and it is often impossible to pin down the responsible party—take steps in preparing your shipment to avoid losses.
- The cost of utilities can skyrocket if you don't take certain steps to streamline your order.
- Sometimes graphics, exhibits and carpet can be damaged during shipment—but there are things you can do to effect temporary repairs on sight.

•Start and maintain a trade show bible—a notebook filled with your knowledge, wisdom and experience in event management. Include problems and solutions, important contact information and details about individual convention centers.

Part 4 - After Words

10
Happily Ever After

Remember Bonnie? The last time we saw her, she was stuck in traffic. It was Monday morning and she had her post show report, which she wrote on the plane ride home. The trade show had been successful in all respects. A happy ending, right?

The truth is, Bonnie's story doesn't have an ending. You see, Bonnie has already started planning next year's trade show. She met with show management, chose a booth space, and signed the contract all before the current show had ended. In fact, she's already mapped out a rough draft of the 12-month countdown. And because Bonnie's company exhibits at several shows every year, she's penciled in items for other shows more than a year in advance.

After she arrives at the office, Bonnie may take a few moments to bask in the glow of a job well done. But there's still plenty of work to be done. The sales department is already processing and following up on the leads gathered at the show.

Bonnie will be busy during the coming weeks, inspecting the exhibit, arranging for repairs. She'll be assessing any problems she had during the show, and look for ways to improve the process. And, she'll plan for the next trade show.

If you've followed the advice and information presented in this book, you're already far ahead of the game. Now it's up to you. What will your post-show report say?

Appendices

Appendix A
Glossary

A

Advertising campaign A set of advertisements with single theme that is repeated over a period of time.

Aisle A walkway for attendees and all others in the convention facility.

Airfreight Goods that are shipped via airplane.

A.T.A.-style flight cases (reusable containers) Reusable containers made of sturdy, light-weight material.

Attendee The people attending the trade show, and who are not associated with the event producer or exhibitors.

Attendee name badge The identification badges that registered attendees must wear in order to gain entrance to the show floor.

B

Backlit graphics A type of translucent graphic that is illuminated from behind.

Backgrounder A sheet of paper containing background information about the company. It usually includes the date the company was founded, names and details about its chief officers, a brief description of the company's products and services, major accomplishments and financial information, if required.

Backwall The panels or draping at the back of the exhibit.

Benefits, product vs. features The positive qualities that are bestowed by the features of a product on the user or consumer. For example, an athletic shoe has Velcro fasteners; that is a feature. The Velcro fasteners make it easier for people with arthritic hands to use the shoes; that is a benefit. Compare with *Features, product vs. benefits.*

"Best of Show" award An award given out at many trade shows, to the product that is judged to excel above others in the same class exhibited at a trade show. To be eligible, a company must submit the product for consideration before the show opens.

Booth An area on the show floor that makes up one or more units of exhibit space.

Booth number The identifying number assigned to a unit of show floor space.

Body language Habits of posture and body movement common to the majority of people that indicate the mood, thinking or inclination of that person. Knowledge of body language is a great tool for salespeople.

Booth staff The people assigned by the exhibitor to work in the booth. Staff can include technical personnel and salespeople.

Business-to-business A term referring to businesses that sell products and services to other businesses.

Business-to-business trade show An event in which the target market are businesses and/or government entities.

C

Central tower The part of a prefabricated exhibit which stands alone, often in or near the center of the booth, and which stands taller than all other components of the exhibit.

Collateral material Printed product information such as brochures, data sheets and catalogues.

Complimentary guest passes Tickets, free of charge, for entrance to the exhibit portion of a trade show. These are available in bulk to exhibitors who want to distribute them to customers and potential customers as an incentive to visit the company's booth.

Consumer trade show An event in which the target market is the end-user, or individuals rather than other businesses.

Convention center A stand-alone facility whose main function is to provide a location and services for conventions, meetings and trade shows.

Convention facilities, hotel A large room in a hotel that provide the necessary facilities for trade shows, exhibitions, conventions and meetings.

Corner booth An exhibit space with exposure on at least two aisles.

Crates Shipping containers, usually made of wood.

Credit card authorization form A form required by all trade show producers that provide valid company credit card information. Exhibitors must settle accounts and pay for all goods and services provided by trade show management by the end of the show. Since most exhibitors continue to accrue charges during the show, show management require a guarantee that the exhibitor

Custom exhibit An exhibit that is designed and constructed for a specific exhibitor/customer.

D

Decision-maker The person, or group of people, with the *authority* or *ability* to approve a purchase.

Demonstration equipment Products that are demonstrated at the trade show.

Dim weight (dimension weight) Standard calculation used by domestic and international transportation companies and agencies to determine the size of the item to be transported. Length x width x height divided by 194 for domestic shipments. Length x width x height divided by 166 for international shipments.

Dimension weight (DIM weight) Standard calculation used by domestic and international transportation companies and agencies to determine the size of the item to be transported. Length x width x height divided by 194 for domestic shipments. Length x width x height divided by 166 for international shipments.

Dismantle (tear-down) The term refers to the taking apart of the exhibit.

Display designers and producers Companies that design and construct trade show exhibits. Use the key phrase "*Display designers and producers*" when performing a global search for exhibit designers and producers on the Internet.

Display products Products that are displayed in the company's exhibit at the trade show.

Direct mail Unsolicited advertising materials delivered by mail.

Drayage The handling of exhibit materials at the trade show. Drayage handlers, usually union laborers hired by convention center, unload exhibit materials from the truck at the loading dock, and transport them to the exhibitor's booth space on the convention center floor.

E

EAC (Exhibitor Appointed Contractor) A contractor, usually a member of a union hired by an exhibitor to perform trade show services independently of show management appointed contractors. The exhibitor must give trade show management and convention center services advance notice of their intention to use an EAC.

Early bird discounts Price discounts on certain services given to exhibitors who order and pay for these services several weeks before the final deadline.

End cap booth (peninsular booth) An exhibit space with aisles on three sides of the booth.

Event producer The company or division that creates, produces and markets the trade show and any associated events.

Exhibit The furniture, graphics, signs, and all other elements of the display.

Exhibitor A company that contracts with the event producer to rent booth space and exhibit at a trade show.

Exhibitor Appointed Contractor (EAC) A contractor, usually a member of a union hired by an exhibitor to perform trade show services independently of show management appointed contractors. The exhibitor must give trade show management and convention center services advance notice of their intention to use an EAC.

Exhibit property A term that refers to the exhibit, particularly the furniture and other structures. Exhibit crafters, designers and producers, and people involved with trade show logistics typically refer to the exhibit as "exhibit property."

Exhibitor badge The name badge that every pre-registered booth staffer must wear at all times, in order to gain access to the trade show floor.

Exhibitor's manual The package of information that contains all information, rules, regulations and forms relating to the trade show. Show management provides the manual, also known as the exhibitor's kit, usually in a three-ring-binder or spiral-bound book.

Exhibitor's kit The package of information that contains all information, rules, regulations and forms relating to the trade show. Show management provides the kit, also known as the exhibitor's manual, usually in a three-ring-binder or spiral-bound book.

Exhibit description form A form provided in the exhibitor's manual, which is used by the exhibitor to describe the nature of the exhibit and the products to be shown. The description that is provided by the exhibitor is used, verbatim, in the *exhibit guide*. Everyone attending the trade show receives a free copy of the *guide*. The exhibit description is a marketing blurb, limited to 50 words or less.

F

Fabrication, exhibit The actual construction of the exhibit.

Fabricator, exhibit The company that builds the exhibit.

Features, product vs. benefits Descriptive facts about a product or service which provide a benefit to the user of the product. See *Benefits, product vs. features*.

Foot traffic The movement of attendees throughout the trade show floor.

Freight handling form A form provided in the exhibitor's manual that allows the exhibitor to describe to the event producer how heavy the exhibitor's shipment will be. This information is provided to the convention center's labor, who must handle the inbound and outbound exhibits.

Frontlit graphics Exhibit graphics that are lighted from the front.

G

Gang box A utility box filled with every conceivable tool, material and supply necessary for setting up the exhibit. Contents can include, but are not limited to: a full set of hand tools, electric screw driver, spare batteries, spare set of keys to exhibit and shipping containers, Velcro (various colors), electrical tape, glue, carpet tape, paint or lacquer (matches exhibit), grease pencils in various colors, spare telephone handset, spare extension cords and electrical power strips.

Guest passes Tickets, free of charge, for entrance to the exhibit portion of a trade show. These are available in bulk to exhibitors who want to distribute them to customers and potential customers as an incentive to visit the company's booth

H

Hand truck Small hand-propelled vehicle used for transporting small loads.

Hanging sign A sign which the exhibitor hangs from the convention center ceiling above the their booth. Certain rules and regulations apply to hanging signs. The exhibitor should always check with the convention center.

Hospitality suite A room or suite which the exhibitor rents at a hotel near the convention center and uses to entertain selected clients, prospects and magazine editors. Ideally, the exhibitor uses the official convention hotel, where the majority of attendees are booked.

I

I&D (Installation & dismantle).. The set up and tear-down of exhibits.

Influencer The person or group within a company that recommends the purchase of a product of service to the decision-maker

In-line booth An exhibit that is constructed in a continuous line along an aisle.

Insertion order form, show guide advertisement The contract for advertising space in the show guide. The exhibitor/advertiser spells out, on the form, the mechanical specifications of the advertisement as well as any special requests, such as where the ad should be placed.

Installation & dismantle (I&D) The set up and tear-down of exhibits.

Island booth An exhibit space open to aisles on all four sides.

K

Kiosk A small physical structure, usually including a computer and display screen, that displays information for people walking by.

Sophisticated kiosks integrate multimedia and include touch screens and video. Some presentations are designed to loop through a series of pages. Other presentations allow the user to interact with it. Advanced designs add Internet access to the presentation.

L

Lanyard A cord attached to an attendee or exhibitor name badge that is worn around the neck.

Leads An inquiry from a qualified prospect. In the context of a trade show, a lead is the paper or electronic record of a prospect's visit to the exhibitor's booth, and subsequent inquiry.

Lead retrieval system A manual or electronic device that allows the exhibitor to collect basic personal information about the prospect. The information includes the prospect's name, company, position, address, phone number and e-mail. The retrieval system can sometimes be programmed to include qualifying information such as product interest, budget and plans to buy.

The prospect's basic information is embossed on his or her name badge. It is also stored on the badge's magnetic strip. A manual retrieval system imprints the embossed information on paper. An electronic system captures information from the magnetic strip.

Liability insurance Insurance that covers the cost of loss or damages to the exhibit, display and demonstration equipment and shipping containers. Trade shoe producers typically offer liability insurance to exhibitors. But many companies find that their own insurance already covers off-site losses.

Lights out request form The form that allows the exhibitor to request that the convention center turn out the hall lights directly above their booth space during the event.

Logo, corporate A specific symbol chosen to represent a company. It is usually comprised of stylized type alone or in conjunction with graphic art.

M

Market A group of people with unsatisfied wants and needs who are willing to purchase and have the means to buy.

Market segment A group of buyers within a market who have relatively similar wants and needs.

Marshaling area An area, lot or parking lotwhere trucks gather for orderly dispatch to show site.

Materials due date, show guide advertisement The date by which all materials to be used to produce and integrate an advertisement into a publication.

Media kit (press kit).. A packet of materials put together for the media. Usually a folder containing news releases (press releases), product announcements, photographic slides, company backgrounder and other materials.

Modular exhibit.. An exhibit constructed with interchangeable components designed to be set up in various arrangements and sizes.

Modular panel system prefabricated exhibit made of rectangular panels designed so that interchangeable panels can be set up in various arrangements and sizes.

Move-in The date specified by show management for beginning exhibit installation. Also called *targeted move-in*.

N

News release (press release) Written news information mailed, faxed or e-mailed to the news media. A good news release contains one primary theme and two or three items or that reinforces the main topic. Most releases announce news about a product, company or individual.

O

Offset printing A printing process in which the inked impression is first made on a rubber roller, and the transferred to paper.

On-line exhibitor's manual A portion of the show producer's web site that is dedicated to a specific show, and which provides most or all of the information and service ordering capabilities contained in the standard "paper" exhibitor's manual.

On-line press room (virtual pressroom, virtual press office) A web site where editors and media professionals can review news releases posted to the site. The virtual press office is an accepted and welcome part of modern public relations. Many trade show producers arrange with a virtual press office to offer free press space for exhibitors to post news releases and artwork.

P

Palette (skid) A low wooden frame used to support heavy objects for easier handling. It is usually used as a platform for objects so that they can be moved by forklift.

Pavilion A set of contiguous booth spaces within a convention center hall occupied by exhibitors whose products and services appeal to a common market segment. For example exhibitors in an Internet pavilion would be companies such as an Internet service provider, a manufacturer of Internet security software and hardware and a manufacturer of modems.

Peninsular booth (end cap booth) An exhibit space with aisles on three sides of the booth.

Pop-up exhibits Lightweight, easy to transport exhibits which can be unpacked, unfolded and set up by one or two people in a matter of minutes. A pop-up can be small enough to fit on a table top, or large enough to provide a ten-foot back wall and graphic.

Prefabricated stock exhibit (stock exhibit) An exhibit that is designed and produced, or fabricated, and ready for rental of purchase by an exhibitor without any modification.

Press conference A collective interview granted to media personnel by a company or its public relations agency.

Press kit (media kit) A packet of materials put together for the media. Usually a folder containing news releases (press releases), product announcements, photographic slides, company backgrounder and other materials.

Press release (news release) Written news information mailed, faxed or e-mailed to the news media. A good news release contains one primary theme and two or three items or that reinforces the main topic. Most releases announce news about a product, company or individual

Press room A room set aside at the convention center by the show producer for the express use of editors and other media professionals. The room is stocked with press kits of various exhibitors, refreshments and a work area. The exhibitor is responsible for making sure a sufficient supply of their media kits (press kits) are placed in the press room.

Priority point system An exhibit space assignment system used by many event producers to provide a fair and balanced method of assigning booth space. The system allows exhibitors to accrue points. The exhibitor with the highest number of points gets to choose their exhibit space before all other exhibitors. The exhibitor with the next highest number of points gets the next choice, and so forth down the line. The company that earns the most priority points gets to select from among the most desired locations on the trade show floor.

Priority points are calculated based on several factors. These include, how many times the company exhibited, consecutively, the company exhibited at the event and how large his was booth space last year

Product locator form The form on which the exhibitor lists all of the types of products and services that he will exhibit at the event. This form goes with the exhibit description form, and is used in the Product Locator section of the show guide.

Prospect A person with the money, authority and desire to buy a product or service; a prospective customer.

Public relations The practice of influencing the media so that they print or broadcast stories that promote favorably, the image of a company, its products and people.

Q

Qualifying leads The act of verifying the value of a lead, wherein the salesperson asks the prospect a series questions based on a predetermined set of criteria.

Quarterly planner A type of wall calendar that displays and entire quarter or a year, or three months, in a single view.

R

Refurbishing, booth/exhibit The process of repairing or reconditioning an exhibit.

Regional trade show A trade show whose market extends to a specific geographical region. For example, an event held in Albany, New York, is aimed at small and medium-size businesses and local governments in the state of New York, and portions of neighboring states.

Reprographics The business of reproducing written or printed materials.

Reusable containers (ATA-style flight cases) Containers used to transport products and exhibits, which can be reused.

S

Service desk The location at the convention center where exhibitors order services from show management

Set-up The process of constructing or erecting the exhibit from its components.

Shipping information form The form the exhibitor uses to tell show management what shipper, trucker or van line it is using to deliver the exhibit, and on what date the shipment will arrive at the convention center.

Show daily (trade show daily) A daily newspaper specific to the trade show, made available to all attendees.

Show guide (trade show guide) A book available to all attendees, that lists each exhibitor along with their booth number and description of their exhibit. Many show guides also provide a cross-reference which exhibitors according to product categories.

Skid (palette) A low wooden frame used to support heavy objects for easier handling. It is usually used as a platform for objects so that they can be moved by forklift.

Specifier The individual or group within a company that defines the qualities and parameters of a particular product or service the company intends to purchase.

Structural graphics, structural exhibit graphics Two- or three dimensional artwork or visual representations that are physically integrated into the exhibit structure.

T

Targeted move-in (target date) The date set by show management for the arrival of the exhibitor's exhibit and equipment at the trade show. Usually, shipments that arrive before this date (and in some instances, after) are assessed a penalty charge.

Talent An individual or company hired to work in an exhibit to greet visitors, demonstrate product, or stage a performance

Tear-down The disassembly and deconstruction of the exhibit into its component parts.

Trade Show bible A set of notes or notebook of useful data and information that the clever, successful trade show manager compiles over the course of his or her career. The information includes, but is certainly not limited to, names and contact information of helpful individuals, notes on various convention centers and cities and trouble-shooting information.

Trade show daily (show guide) A daily newspaper specific to the trade show, made available to all attendees.

Trade show guide (show guide) A book available to all attendees, that lists each exhibitor along with their booth number and description of their exhibit. Many show guides also provide a cross-reference which exhibitors according to product categories

V

Video wall One or more video displays that allow the exhibitor to deliver a variety of advertising or marketing messages to an audience. The audience can be several yards or several aisles away, depending on the size and complexity of the wall. Video walls that use several displays.

Virtual trade show A trade show produced and presented on the world wide web. Many event producers are providing virtual trade shows as a part of their live events.

Virtual press office (on-line press room) A web site where editors and media professionals can review news releases posted to the site. The virtual press office is an accepted and welcome part of modern public relations. Many trade show producers arrange with a virtual press office to offer free press space for exhibitors to post news releases and artwork.

Y

Yearly planner A type of wall calendar that displays an entire year in a single view

Appendix B

Resources

Organizations

The Trade Show Exhibitor's Association (TSEA). An organization for trade show professionals that provides knowledge to marketing and management types who use exhibits to promote and sell their products. 5501 Backlick Road, Suite 105, Springfield, VA 22151, (703) 941-3725, e-mail tsea@tsea.org, web www.tsea.org.

Information on the Web

www2.tsnn.com. Trade Show News Network—The Ultimate Trade Show Resource. Excellent web site with comprehensive information on all aspects of trade show exhibiting including exhibit sales, service suppliers, event listings and industry news. The site also provides a wonderful list of professional organizations broken down by industry.

www.tsea.org. The web site for The Trade Show Exhibitor's Association (TSEA) an organization for trade show professionals. The organization offers its members job connections and educational opportunities.

www.PubList.com. The Internet directory of publications. A free database of over 150,000 magazines, journals, newsletters and other periodicals, national and international.

Industry Periodicals

Exhibit Marketing Magazine. Eaton Hall Publishing, 256 Columbia Turnpike, Florham Park, New Jersey, 07932, (800) 746-9646.

Exhibitor. Exhibitor Magazine Group, 206 S. Broadway, Suite. 745, Rochester, MN, 55904-6565. (888) 235-6155, E-mail exmag@isl.net, web www.exhibitornet.com.

Tradeshow Week. Tradeshow Week, 5700 Wilshire Blvd., Suite 120, Los Angeles, CA. 90036-5804, (323) 965-5333. weekly source of news & statistics on the tradeshow industry Web www.tradeshowweek.com

Service Providers

Exhibit Manufacturers

MICE DisplayWorks. A designer and manufacturer of trade show exhibits. 6489 Oak Canyon, Irvine, CA 92618-5202, toll-free 800-441-8895, telephone 949-654-0401, fax 949-654-0400. www.displayworks.com.

Exhibitgroup/Giltspur. A division of the Viad Corporation. 200 North Gary Avenue, Roselle, IL 60172, (800) 307-2400, (630) 307-2400. www.e-g.com.

Nomadic Displays. A producer of portable and modular displays. 7400 Fullerton Road, Suite 134, Springfield, VA, 22153 (703) 866-9200, www.nomadicdisplay.com.

Skyline Displays, Inc. 3355 Discovery Road, Eagan, MN 55121, (800) 328-2725. Web www.skylinedisplays.com.

Recommended Reading

Bly, Robert W. *The Copywriter's Handbook*. New York: Henry Holt and Company, 1990

Covey, Stephen R. First Things First. New York: Simon & Schuster, 1995.

Covey, Stephen R. *The 7 Habits of Highly Effective People*. New York: Simon & Schuster, 1990.

Girard, Joe. *How to Sell Yourself*. New York: Warner Books, 1992

Levinson, Jay Conrad, Mark S.A. Smith, and Orvel Ray Wilson. *Guerrilla Trade Show Selling*. New York: John Wiley & Sons, Inc. 1997.

McGaulley, Michael T. *Selling 101: Essential Selling Skills for Business Owners and Non-salespeople*. Holbrook, Massachusetts: Adams Media Corporation, 1995

Miller, Stephen. *How to Get the Most Out of Trade Shows*. Chicago: NTC Business Books, 2000.

Misner, Ivan R. Ph.D. and Don Morgan, M.A. *Masters of Networking: Building Relationships for Your Pocketbook and Soul*. Marietta, Georgia: Bard Press, 2000.

RoAne, Susan. *The Secrets of Savvy Networking: How to Make the Best Connections for Business and Personal Success*. New York: Warner Books, 1993.

Index

C

M

N

O